AUGURY

AUGURY

PHILIP GARRISON

THE UNIVERSITY OF GEORGIA PRESS

ATHENS AND LONDON

© 1991 by Philip Garrison

Published by the University of Georgia Press

Athens, Georgia 30602

All rights reserved

Designed by Louise M. Jones

Set in 10/13 Meridien

The paper in this book meets the guidelines for
permanence and durability of the Committee on
Production Guidelines for Book Longevity of the
Council on Library Resources.

Printed in the United States of America

95 94 93 92 91   5 4 3 2 1

Library of Congress Cataloging in Publication Data

Garrison, Philip.

Augury / Philip Garrison.

p.   cm.

ISBN 0-8203-1312-2 (alk. paper)

I. Title.

PS3557.A74A94   1991

814'.54—dc20   90-11255   CIP

British Library Cataloging in Publication Data available

For Patricia

The publication of this book is supported by a grant from the National Endowment for the Arts, a federal agency.

CONTENTS

FOREWORD

Nineteenth-century psychologists spent massive amounts of time trying to understand acts of attention. This was the heyday of compulsory education and their interests were largely pedagogical as they designed ingenious experiments to measure and improve the human attention span. It irked them that children had such a small one. A single imperative rang throughout American classrooms: "Pay attention!" What to do about all this mind-wandering and wool-gathering, all this absent-mindedness that the French call *distraction*? Young minds should be trained not to wander. So these early psychologists invented mental regimens equivalent to the splash of ice-cold water clergymen recommended to combat wayward thoughts. The psychologists even found the clue to genius: it was largely a matter of focused attention, intense concentration, superior mental efficiency.

Philip Garrison's essays remind us of what a peculiar thing

attention is and how much we can lose in our determination to focus it. To pay attention—in the classroom's strictest sense— too often entails a restraint of vision, a loss of what's happening at the edges of concepts and consciousness. In Garrison's writing, the edges are as real as the center, though this geometric distinction usually gets blurred in the tensions of perception that inform his essays. *Augury* opens with an appropriate image: "The window frame bulges with blue sky." The essay is also a frame; and in Garrison's hands its edges bulge.

The window frame is an enduring symbol of perceptual boundaries. Look at the paintings of Edward Hopper; they are full of windows, windows abutting windows. And there are the more elegant windows of Virginia Woolf. But Garrison has found an even better, more suitable device for his imagination—the windshield. A moving frame, the windshield blurs and fragments perceptions. And unlike a window, a windshield is designed for peripheral vision. In "Three Days in the Mexican Highlands," Garrison notices a countryside of "disparate signals, incompatible emblems." No matter how hard we attend to this landscape, it "offers no interpretive key, no central place from which to observe it, no unquivering pivot from which the different blurs resolve into figure and ground." We are observing here not a mountainside but the dynamics of attention. "Whichever direction we look, the focus of attention seems to lie way beyond our windshield." There is no center the eye can hold on to. "Wherever we stop, the countryside is all border, boundary, edge and rim. So we keep on driving through it." Like an essay submitting to its author's distractions, a windshield can become the locus of odd juxtapositions. In a Mexican bus ("Tombs"), Garrison notices that the driver has placed above the windshield two images—a bronze crucifix and a pornographic photo. These icons "wring a certain equilibrium out of whatever image fills the windshield."

Most of these essays are set in Mexico, and the theme of borders runs throughout the collection. For Garrison, Mexico is ripe territory for what he calls "figure ground reversals," the country continually opening to "cognitive dissonance." There seems to be no way to come to terms with the place: "Each of our observations has felt half-transitional, a dip of attention from one act of noticing to another, our each perception throwing some other into a momentary clarity" ("Borders"). These are not travel essays in any conventional sense. Though Garrison is very much at home in Mexico, he doesn't—despite years of experiences and excursions—pretend to "know" it. His essays have none of that ironic superiority to tourists that spoils the tone of so much contemporary travel literature.

Whether Garrison is seeking sanctuary in an old railroad tunnel, visiting the Grand Coulee Dam (when's the last time anyone's written about *that*?), participating in a peyote pilgrimage, meditating on obscure superstitions, discussing the classics, or riding in the back seat of a Mexican patrol car looking for wrecks, he shows a remarkable capacity to let his thoughts and observations melt into a penumbra of relations, as one act of attention passes into the fringe of another. "Boundary Loss" is what Rorschach specialists call the inability to see definite images in fuzzy ink blots, as though the knack of finding borders and outlines represents human perception at its peak.

Augurers, too, are attentive to blurred boundaries: the shifting patterns of oil on water, the shape of clouds, the configuration of birds in flight, a chance expression that might turn out to be an epiphany. Augurers, as Garrison is aware, have a way of catching the momentary transition or fleeting relation that ordinary people—their attention focused only on what's in front of them—too easily miss. In the rhetoric of augury, we are never sure what the topic is; what something's "about" is more a matter of contiguity than identity.

I love Philip Garrison's essays for what they *don't* know. His is an essential American voice intent on exploring a geographical—and mental—landscape of indefinite borders. Like William James, Garrison believes that "life is in the transitions," and at the heart of *Augury* is a deep intellectual respect for the inter-rupted moment, the quirky experience, the mysterious friend-ship, the observations that don't add up. These are essays in the best tradition of American reflection.

Robert Atwan

ACKNOWLEDGMENTS

I appreciate the financial support granted by Central Washington University's Faculty Research Committee. My thanks go to the editors of the journals where some of these essays, in these or slightly different forms, first appeared.

Colorado Review: "The Republic of Boylston"
High Plains Literary Review: "Monument"
North American Review: "Adaptations"
Northwest Review: "American Miracles," "Borders," "Independence Day," "The Tour Guide," "Two Love Scenes in Homer," "Where Pigs Can See the Wind"
Puerto del Sol: "Burning What We Weave," "Finding Our Lives"

AUGURY

INDEPENDENCE
DAY

The window frame bulges with blue sky. I'm on floor six, in a hotel called the De Luxe, in Cd. Juárez, in Mexico. Alone, a bit hung over from the night before, I've returned to a town I visited first some twenty-five years ago. A year ago nearly to the day, I shared this room with my wife, vacationing. But now I've come here to be alone, to get some rest. For the last six months, beginning with the death of my father, my own emotions have shaken me back and forth, as if by the neck. I've gone from feeling hurt to feeling hopeful, from foolish to fearful. As I think of how he died, swollen from chemotherapy, the cancer leaking upward in him like tiny bubbles, from prostate to lungs, I stub out another of the cigarettes that I've started smoking again. As I write, my hand trembles with the strain of having carried a heavy suitcase from the downtown El Paso bridge to where I now perch, looking north, thinking back.

I took a taxi for the last six blocks. The driver, a man my father's age, chatted with the resigned, half-disdainful aplomb of the elderly Mexican male. Yes, it snows nearly every winter here. No, a person can't make ends meet nowadays. . . . He lets me off at the hotel's front door. I get a room and spend an hour walking streets I recall from a quarter-century ago. The auto exhaust and tourist bars, the curio shops and money-changing houses, they all bring back emotions I never quite can recapture unless I'm here. In the hall corridor hangs a 1923 photo of Pancho Villa, shot dead in his convertible. He dangles upside down, over the driver's door, hands flung out as if addressing a crowd.

By dark I'm sitting in the Kentucky Club Bar, pink neon windows reflecting off fenders at the curb, Glenn Miller songs in the air. The oak backbar must be a hundred years old. On the wall hang photos of Jack Johnson and Gene Tunney, doubling their fists at their own autographs. "Moonlight Serenade" and "Pennsylvania 6-5000" keep floating over the clink of glass, the hum of small talk. They remind me of my father. He would have heard them in the early forties, coming home dirty and tired from slinging tires at the Goodyear plant in Springfield, Missouri, the wartime job he got put to performing when a nearly blind right eye exempted him from military service. I don't remember much of those days: he comes home in a dirty T-shirt, he sleeps a lot; and my mother is frequently cross. Even by then, I guess, they were quarreling about his drinking.

In the earliest memory I have, I'm running from him. I must be about two. I'm weaving in and out of traffic in the street, dodging headlights. I can hear him gaining on me, those huge footsteps drawing nearer. And there the scene freezes, with neither beginning nor end. I'm sure he caught me, sure we went back to the house. I must have been pretty scared. And yet, as part to whole, that fuzzy memory recapitulates the entire connection between us: I could never bring him into focus. He always seemed a blurred series of transitions, a flurry of emotions I could neither make friends with nor fight, but only flee. Changeable as weather, his moods followed a logic I could separate, at best, into something like "seasons." By turns sentimental and stoic, he'd train either attacks or tears on me. He'd seem generous, then stingy, sympathetic, then aloof. Often I was positive he had multiple personalities; but none of them had anything at all to do with me, with what I had done or was doing. We might talk, all alone, for as long as an hour; but he always seemed to be addressing someone else. I occasioned the words he appeared to aim past me, out into empty space. I never felt I was more than the simple, mechanical cause of what he was saying, a pretext he would seize, at times I couldn't predict, to make remarks so heavily coded that I only now begin to get their sense.

Behind his words, by now, I can hear his needs, insistent, mercurial. And tonight, walking back to my hotel room, I suddenly realize how often it is that I'm thinking of him this weekend. Here on the Juárez sidewalks, fifteen hundred miles from the Mississippi River town we shared, six months after I buried him, I'm terribly tired of him. He and I need a break from each other. Each of us has to get free of the other's scrutiny.

Skyrockets splash red and green and white against the night sky my hotel window frames. They remind me that Mexico, this weekend, celebrates 179 years of existence as a republic. Each muffled thud flings the colors of the national flag hundreds of feet in the air over the Franklin Mountains, above their twinkling radio towers. Some of the explosions glitter and blink out; others spread garish petals that droop and fade. I can't decide from my window whether the source of all this display is here in Juárez, or in El Paso, across the river. Red for the blood of heroes. Green for the soil's fertility. White for the purity of, what is it they like to say? I doze off watching patriotic spurts of light.

Daylight returns pigeons and crows to the rooftops. The building below my window, festooned with green and red pennants, has painted across the front of it, in letters three feet high, *Partido Revolucionario Institucional*. In the hotel dining room, I breakfast on *chilaquiles* and mineral water, beside a table of three cops yawning, gossiping. By ten in the morning, I'm waiting on

Insurgentes Avenue for the Independence Day parade to pass. I perch on a fence on the corner across from the reviewing stand. To my left stands the Division General Francisco Villa Prep School, and to the right, a small shopping center. Out of a huge loudspeaker, below the empty chairs on the stand, flows a continuous stream of love songs. Vendors sell popsicles colored red and green and white. A line of uniformed cops, shoulder to shoulder, guards the curb the length of the block. From the tip of a popsicle stick, one of them sucks a last lump of red slush, bowing the stick between thumb and forefinger. Flipping it at a manhole cover ten feet away, he misses and giggles.

A chair at a time, the reviewing stand fills up. Announcing the parade's progress toward us, block by block, the loudspeaker interrupts the love songs with a deep, impersonal voice, a voice trained on years of official remarks, on thousands of standardized feelings. Endlessly, it reassures us that *aquí en donde empieza y termina la patria, festejamos 179 años de la independencia:* here where our land begins and ends, we celebrate 179 years of independence. I study the dozen or so men in *guayaberas* and army uniforms slouched on the reviewing stand. From which of them is the voice proceeding? Hard to tell.

Suddenly, a skinny woman in a cheap jogging suit, an arm's length to the right of me, groans and pitches backward, clipping the base of her skull on the curb with a sound that turns my stomach. She groans again and begins to writhe with what looks like an epileptic seizure. While a man who seems to be her husband lifts her to a sitting position, I slip my belt between her teeth to keep her from biting her tongue. Out of an inner distance, ambiguous as that from which the mechanical voice proceeds—vibrating all about me—I can feel, more than hear, my father's disapproval of these people. He never could hide his distaste for this side of the border. The people are lazy, and have too many children. They're dirty and poor and superstitious. . . . Meanwhile I'm half-amazed, lifting her in my arms, at how little she weighs. Her husband opens the door of the ambulance that's arrived, and hands me my belt. I notice his fingernails are dirty. As they drive off, my shirt front smells as if her hair hadn't been washed for days.

The parade trickles by. Every prep-school marching band in the city must be in it. Teenage girls in black wool slacks and tunics tramp, saluting and sweating, to the foot of Benito Juárez's fifty-foot memorial column. As I wander off among them, I can feel my father's surveillance lessen, his outrage diminish, as if I could leave him behind by turning a corner, cutting down an alley, crossing a street. Waiters and clerks keep wanting to practice their English on me. But when I reply, they can't follow. While they heave a disappointed shrug, returning to Spanish, I wince at the futility animating their features. The whole landscape takes on an air of futility: the graceful monuments, spray painted with graffiti, and then scrubbed, and then sprayed again; the well-designed park benches, with half their seats pried off; the creek diverted to run through a park, but clogged with throw-away diapers.

I realize once again, for what has to be the thousandth time in my life, how thoroughly this side of the border blends the grotesque and the graceful, the elegant and the disgusting. A certain detachment, understandably, characterizes the way Mexicans pass from childhood to old age. The country's wry incongruities seem to find their patron in the image of the Virgin of Zapopan, her seventeenth-century porcelain head, her cornhusk body clad in rare silks and jewels. Once a year she tours in a Ford Galaxy the faithful pull through the streets of Guadalajara, ropes attached to the axles. . . . Deep and inexplicable contrasts bind these people together. It's always made a special kind of sense to me that they call what they are, collectively, *la patria*, the fatherland.

My father couldn't bear Mexico. I think it aroused in him what it does in everyone else: a mix of feelings as garish as they are powerful. The force and unpredictability of his mood swings, year after year, had left him desperate to control his least emotion. On both of the brief visits he ever managed to this side of the border, I saw him flinch, when sitting down to supper, at the brilliant paper flowers at his elbow, and then at a ragged shoeshine boy at his feet. He might have kept on trying to tolerate this country, if only because it had become so important to me; but his illness, the last few years of his life, left him ever more vulnerable to himself.

The last trip we went on together reminded me just why it was he'd spent his life in Missouri, or downstate Illinois, eating middle western food and voting for drab Republicans, living every year through four distinct seasons, worshiping his God with tithes as regular as clockwork. The day we rented a jet to fly him to Houston, for chemotherapy, he lay on a stretcher in back, beside him a male nurse in a sky-blue jumpsuit. My mother and I crouched in seats in front. Below us, in slow motion, there dropped away the blond, rolling November corn fields he never would see again. The flight took six hours. Like a flat rock skipped over water, we glided and dipped across turbulence. As I watched him doze, cheekbone pressing windowpane, I began to understand how much he always had needed bland surroundings. The clouds all around us, edgeless, endless, must've seemed an improvement on even the rolling hills he was used to. Nothing too abrupt, no transition too jagged, threatened the composure gripping his face.

By sundown the streets of Juárez have cooled. Shadows draw a gratifying chill out of the desert. For dinner I meet a friend who lives in El Paso. As we eat, we talk about Mexico, our conversation sustained by the street outside, the air wrinkling with auto exhaust, lime rinds green in the gutter, an endless line of girls in stretch pants and eyeshadow passing a church's facade. We ease out of the restaurant and into two or three saloons, drinking, smoking. After awhile my friend has to leave, to get up in time for work tomorrow. I'm left in the bar below my hotel room, finishing a tequila. And then I'm upstairs in front of my window.

My father did the actual drinking, when I was young. The rest of us lived as codependents, conspiring to hide our terror of him, our guilt that we couldn't make him stop acting the very way that, before long, we needed him to act. When his feelings gyrated so fiercely, the only way we could live in peace became to anticipate what he wanted, before he himself knew what it was. However much we resented it, we had to interpret his words and deeds to find out what they meant. Denying that we felt any resentment lent our lives, after awhile, the tranquillity his mood swings needed. Lying became our way of life: he demanded a semblance of normalcy; and we demanded that he demand it. How could we bear for people to know our complicity? We needed the threat of his displeasure, his promise of unpredictability, to keep our words full of the neutral content that excused the way we lived.

It was in reaction to that neutrality, I think, that emotional speech became for me the most important kind of experience. I can't recall a time that I wasn't hungry for passionate words. My mouth pursued them the way the mouths of the drowning go after air. Words could wring laughter or tears out of adults whose attention went right through me as if I were glass. I needed words to tickle or slap or caress. Now I realize why, when I was young, and leaving my father's part of the country, I headed straight for this side of the border: it felt like a powerful kind of speech. Mexico, like words themselves, yielded feelings so lurid and lovely that no one dared deny its existence.

By now there's moonlight all over the spray-painted statues, the broken sidewalks. This drooping, heavyset Mexican moon brings back the night that my father died. I was up in Colorado, seeing a few friends. From Houston my sister called, to say that he had maybe a day left. It could be that his doctors had miscalculated his strength. Or maybe his willpower wore out. Anyhow, I took off on a bus for Denver, to fly to Houston. When he died, I was riding that bus. I still had the airport to get to, and the night to pass in an airport chair, waiting for the earliest flight I could get. I managed afterward to ask a lot of questions, to find out when it was that he quit breathing. And he and I, it turns out, were having a little chat in the back of that bus at that very moment.

There I was heading down back roads, from Fort Collins to Denver, sucking the pint of tequila I bought to numb what I knew I'd feel. For as far as I could see in every direction, moonlight covered the fields and the sheds. All of this country had been Mexican, even five hundred years before tonight, even if they did call it Aztlán. I felt him say that we probably needed to tell each other goodbye. I said I didn't want to. He said that from then on, every time I looked at the moon, whatever thought came to my mind, that could be his way of talking to me. Wanting him not to leave, I joked that the moon was feminine, by tradition anyhow. But hadn't I ever heard of the man in the moon? he wanted to know. He said that when I saw the moon I'd think of him, at least. I said I figured I would.

His funeral, a week later, amounted to a kind of anticlimax. Back and forth, from the chapel pew to the roses spread over his polished casket, my mother kept exercising a strange, stiff-legged control, gasping into a handkerchief. My sister and I kept striding purposefully away, then edging back, to say goodbye again: the morticians had slipped one of his big, bony hands into the other, as if he were leading himself across a dangerous intersection. At last they screwed the lid down, and slid back the room divider, so that we could shake hands with those who'd known him, and those who hadn't.

Although he hadn't been active in the organization for years, my mother buried him in a Shriner's fez. Three months of chemotherapy had cost him all his hair. And so he went off to meet his god wearing that bit of Egyptian headgear acclimated long since to the social nuances of the American Middle West. His wearing it indicated, equally, the strength with which he had fought for his life, and mother's indecision about leaving the casket open. Even after she decided at last to close the lid to the public, she had them leave the fez on his head, as if to help the three of us remember he had departed this earth under protest. I couldn't take my eyes off him. The sequins sewn on the felt in the shape of a scimitar glittered with incongruity. But that wouldn't have mattered to him. Incongruity never had been a feature to which he much responded.

Indeed his whole life, now that it was over, seemed a montage of beginnings and ends, an exercise in unlikelihood, a blend of the incompatible with the indeterminate. One of five children, my father was by nine years the youngest. Born to surprised, delighted parents already in their forties, he never during his infancy spent a single night in a crib. He slept between his mother and father, and felt their gratitude for his existence follow him about, lending his every word and step a kind of heightened importance, all through childhood, and then adolescence. At age twenty-five, winning the hand of the pretty schoolteacher he courted, he set out promptly to conceive a son. But she wasn't, it seemed at first, well suited to childbearing: miscarriages frustrated their plans, again and again. So when I became their firstborn, I not only represented a certain tension knotted between them. I also amounted to a demand made upon him, something expected of him by that audience he felt observing his life.

To this day, I have no idea when it was that his job started to hurt him. Probably any line of work would've felt monotonous, peripheral to all that focus trained on him while he was growing up. Maybe no matter what he'd done for a living, a certain amount of drinking would've had to ease his growing lack of definition, his feeling that his life was dwindling to an uninterrupted stream of transitions. But now as I stood beside his casket, shaking hands with his friends, I realized that he and they truly were transitional figures, both to themselves and to each other: the Great Depression had pretty much severed the continuity of their lives. All of them grew up as farm boys. Hard times had uprooted them, had left them selling livestock feed or life insurance, shelving groceries maybe, but praising God no matter what. They had to, after all. Their belief lent their lives a certain supple substratum. The soul was a continuity that let a fellow explain himself to himself: some immortal, measureless part persisted through whatever kind of luck might befall him. So the sequins and velvet in that casket did indicate, if only by chance, the degree to which God himself had served my father's adult years as audience.

Long before he died, he'd pretty well quit drinking. But years of estrangement already separated us. When I visited, during his last months, our conversations would swoop and dip all around his hospital room, touching on any topic but the scar tissue grown between us, the pain we'd avoided mentioning for nearly half a century. Each would feel the other approaching a raw nerve, and flinch. At one point he said he regretted never having given me the benefit of all of his experience. But how do you know you haven't? I protested. It's kind of like my own father used to say, he smiled: the gun kicks harder when you hit the squirrel. . . . We went back and forth that way, probing, parrying like tired fighters, or tired lovers.

By now I can see that I've done it again. I've put in one more aimless night, interpreting what was my last view of him, convinced that he lay in his casket with all the meaning of a handwritten note, some bit of advice he slipped me from the other side of one of those preoccupied moods of his. I came here planning to forget him for awhile, to hide out. Mexican Independence Day seemed the perfect occasion to declare my own emotional autonomy. And then, within hours, I was wondering where better than right here, the edge of a land riddled with incongruities, to begin sorting out his contradictions. If any place could, Mexico would throw him into meaningful relief. After all, hadn't my father even been born on November 2, the Day of the Dead? . . . Step by step, it turns transparent, the way he makes me his audience, then keeps me trying to figure him out. His fortunes become mine, as if he were a fictional character unfurling before me. I've even wound up mimicking his compulsions: the drinking that left him talking right through me; the cigarette smoking that killed him, and left me eyeing him like a page.

It's morning. My bag is packed. I slip a still-damp toothbrush into my shaving kit, and head downstairs to where the desk clerk's son is ready, in a pickup, to drive me to the airport. He's maybe twenty, slender and polite. His father, it turns out, was born in Santa Barbara. The streets are empty at this hour. Every time I see it, I realize that I've forgotten again how the fence on the international bridge bends, at the top, at a nasty, oblique angle. It reminds me how the United States means to discourage even the most avid prospective immigrant, even somebody willing to jump a hundred feet to the river trickling under us, down its concrete trough.

ADAPTATIONS

At the moment, Manastash Creek couldn't get any fuller. Cold, shallow, twisting over boulders and red grass, full of whitecaps clinging to dips, of sandbars dimpling it with eddies, the water's very little warmer than the snow it used to be, ten miles north, where it melted off the Cascade peaks we can see on a clear day. It splashes down sagebrush slopes. It meanders between salt blocks set out for deer, under the boughs of willow and aspen that quail roost in, over the worn-out tractor tires tossed off concrete farm-road bridges. The sound, at twenty feet, resembles that of someone gargling. At fifty feet, from my yard spotted with violets and deer tracks, it blends into that steady s-s-s-h-h-h produced by the smooth rocks it tumbles, spring by spring, farther down the trail some glacier left from here to the river.

Two hundred yards from my front door, in the middle of what is now a corn field, there once stood a log cabin. In it, a hundred years ago, the grandmother of a friend of mine was born to pioneer parents. When my friend was a child, he'd fall asleep at night hearing his grandmother tell how hard it'd been to get to sleep, when she herself was a child, lying on her straw tick, listening to the cough and shriek of cougars hunting down by the river.

Today, in many ways, the valley remains what it was a century ago. Coyotes still skulk in the sagebrush. Deer still browse on creek-bank willow leaves. In fact, practically anywhere we look, the eye lights on some reminder of that decade, a hundred years ago, when Euro-America set about dividing this ancient lake bed into homesteads and ranches, pastures and hay fields. Up and down my end of the valley, for example, roads swerve back and forth for no apparent reason. Maybe some farmer wouldn't give up the right-of-way. Or maybe the county took advantage of preexisting paths, trails, lanes. Only the first settlers could've said what fits of envy or pride, or what degrees of convenience, left each road dodging the way it does across our utterly level valley floor. Sometimes our roads proceed as if they were zigzagging, full of switchbacks, as if they were climbing one of the steep ridges that surround us, on all sides, cutting off sunlight, funneling wind over us, northwest to southeast.

I wonder how the settlers would have explained our twisting roads. Much of what they had to say about this valley survives in the form of interviews, or oral autobiographies, reminiscences transcribed more than half a century ago. By the time local pioneers got around to telling their tales, the depression had arrived. I like to imagine them chatting on some front porch, surrounded by WPA interviewers, these men and women in their eighties, a lot of them born on the Oregon Trail, in the 1850s or 1860s.

Back and forth in their memories play images of the endless plains, as well as of some huge, uncut forest they found. They describe themselves perching on a prairie horizon, or huddling in little clearings they pried apart in all that green virgin inertia. They peek outdoors, through windowpanes that Yankee clippers fetched around the Horn. To get through one fierce bliz-

13

zard, they burn the fence poles they spent all summer cutting. They even empty the straw from their bed ticks and burn it. But fevers and chills run through their bodies, regardless. The soil starts to embrace their dead in narrow, choirlike rows.

Some of my favorite pioneer tales amount to heirlooms, really. Even though they relate events that happened to the first generation to arrive here, the narratives themselves got collected from that generation's children, or from its grandchildren. Consider the story about the little old lady who had green hair. Someone's grandmother once took it in mind to dye her white wavy locks the same brown that the walnut husks she boiled had stained her hands. But the water she poured over her hair turned it, instead, the bright green of walnut shells. She couldn't get rid of the color. She had to let it grow out. And me, I have to admire how that story kept on retelling itself. Persistent as Manastash Creek, it adapted to the psychic terrain of different generations, flowing around and through however many births and deaths there were that got in the way.

Even today we can see these pioneers glaring out of family portraits, boots and bonnets quaint, fists and jaws clenched against the uncertainty of life out here. Their voices turn suddenly proud, at even the most temporary victories: a hatful of fresh-dug potatoes, the quilt they've sewed, the horsehair bridle they've braided. The whole landscape, in surrounding it, seems to adapt to each little homestead. Glacial valleys quote what people shout at each other. When forest fires singe the sky, chickens roost at noon; sidewalks, riding out an earthquake, writhe like snakes. Within a single generation, towns are getting named for whatever sprouts or flows nearby.

A human generation is maybe twenty or thirty years. And yet, to the sagebrush out my window, *Artemisia tridentata,* twenty or thirty years amount to no time at all. Any individual plant may live a century or more. They just keep inching along, downward, outward. The snow one winter may blow in from Siberia. The rain, next spring, might get wrung from the Amazon. And yet, as if they were huge, underground wings, my sagebrush continues unfurling its thirty-foot roots. It devotes all its probing, deliberate guesswork to staying alive.

The name Artemisia belonged to a sad queen of Halicarnassus. She named and identified herbs. She married her brother and, when he died, insisted that the world share her grief: the tomb she ordered for him took years to complete, because she kept changing her mind, wanting it larger, grander. Even while being built, it got to be so famous that it turned into one of the ancient world's seven wonders. The name of her brother was Mausolus. Her passion for him reaches our ears in the form of the word "mausoleum."

Like the pride and grief of that poor queen, the sagebrush plants out my window thrive by accommodating themselves to changing circumstances, projecting in all directions their different versions, their adaptations. Cousin to the wormwood that flavors both absinthe and gall, sagebrush grows all over the world, in one form or another: South Africa, South America, the western United States and the Asiatic steppes. Mugwort, motherwort, southernwood, tarragon, 280 species of low shrubs, of bitter-aromatic herbs, cover arid regions of the world, their leaves dividing frequently, their flowers inconspicuous. The first settlers in this valley counted on the presence of sagebrush to tell them where the soil was free enough of alkali to plant crops.

The sagebrush out my window grows in a peculiar way. Maybe it owes to the sheer force the plant has to exert, converting scant winter rain into growth rings. Down where the bark goes gray, and begins to unravel, the trunk grows by splaying itself apart. When I stand directly above it, looking down, the individual plant resembles a burst of wooden rays released by the ground.

Underneath the sagebrush branches, up and down the creek bank, adult quail flicker. Like tiny shadows, their chicks follow them. The average individual lives a little less than ten months, with only one in several hundred surviving five years. By day the covey dissolves into couples, reassembling at roosting time. This time of year, when May greens the diet, threat and love call alike train the voice. Social life amounts to imitating whatever behavior it is that lets the covey survive: the young learn to freeze or to flush from adults made furtive by the awkwardness of the young.

At a certain remove, a quail covey resembles a kind of story, a tale told in a flesh-and-feather medium. The principal antagonists are food supply and the reproductive urge. Fewer adults mate during the years there's little nourishment, and more mate during years of plenty: the numbers of the population diminish and intensify, like a plot. But our hunting them also plays a role in the story. And for our part, a lot of the way that we have always lived, here in the intermontane West, has owed to our taste for their flesh. Seventy-five generations ago, for example, men wove half-mile traps of human hair to snare them. Topknots of the males decorated basket lid and sleeve. Women would dry the flesh, or pound it up with salt. They'd boil the eggs by dropping hot stones into baskets full of water. Or wrap them in grass and bake them in ashes. Teenage girls wouldn't eat quail for fear they'd nest in their hair. Grandmothers swore that quail spent the daylight hours underground, gambling for the souls of the dead.

The coyotes that lurk out there in the sagebrush represent another story the floor of this valley is telling. No mammal knows better how to adapt, to cooperate with other life forms: coyotes will wait at the exit of the prairie-dog tunnel that a badger is demolishing; they'll scavenge calf droppings for the undigested milk; they'll nose the tracks of elk, in deep snow, for mice. When cowboys on Texas trail drives, back in the 1870s, shot the newborn calves that couldn't keep up, guess who followed for hundreds of miles, singing and feasting?

The behavior of the coyote seems unpredictable as that of luck itself. They've been observed eating bumblebees and watermelons, butterflies and rattlesnakes: help in staying alive can come from any direction. It was Richard M. Nixon, fittingly enough, who issued an order forbidding the poisoning of coyotes on federal land. (Some people even say that they fish with their tails for crab or shrimp.) No wonder the Navajo call the coyote "god's dog."

Puking up food for the pups, rubbing the muzzle clean on grass, the coyote is going to stay alive at all costs. Four of every five die in their first year, and only 12 percent live to reproduce. But thirteen subspecies range from Alaska to Guatemala.

For most of the generations humans have spent in this valley, we've believed that a coyote brought it into being. Most of the people to live here have belonged to one of various native American cultures, hunter-gatherer folk who always attributed the qualities of this place to the whimsical nature of Coyote, its creator. The stories they tell about him are endless. In nobody knows how many languages, he sulks and pouts, throws tantrums or grieves, falls in love or flies into a rage. And every mishap sets a precedent, explains why our lives are arbitrary, brief, and often painful. Everyone seems always to have known the stories were ancient: for a very long time, life in this valley has been the way those stories describe it.

So when Euro-American settlers appeared, Indians couldn't answer a lot of the crazy questions they got asked. They couldn't say, for example, exactly how long it'd been that they'd been digging camas and hunting deer. Some of them, to hunt buffalo, would ride hundreds of miles east. They'd even go after bulls, the big ones that gore a man's horse and, while the hunter plays dead on the ground, lick his face raw for the salt on it. But no, they couldn't really say how long life had been like this. They only knew that, ever since they collectively could remember, they'd spent part of their lives hiding in out-of-the-way places, singing and fasting for magic. And now the appearance of white people seemed to represent a trial, a test of whether the Power they'd acquired could adapt.

The Indians' equivalent to the pioneer tales I admire are their own oral autobiographies, taken down early in this century, from elderly men and women who, when young, had resisted Euro-America's invasion of their lands. Several Nez Percé stories relate the time a one-armed Quaker general came to drive them back onto a reservation. The survivors' accounts explain that those who took arms, and fled, called themselves the Dreamers. Traditional visionaries, devoted to the hunter-gatherer life, they refused to farm alongside their Presbyterian Nez Percé neighbors.

At White Bird Canyon, Fire Body dropped the army bugler from fifty yards away. Altogether, the Dreamers killed thirty-three soldiers, and threatened the Christian Nez Percé scouts with a hazel-switch whipping if they pursued. Then they vanished: they crossed the Salmon River by lashing buffalo robes to green willow poles, hair side up, to make hide boats. Somewhere down the trail, they found a trooper still alive, shot between the eyes, and through the breast, face washed in his own blood. He made a clucking sound like a hen. No one wanted to kill him, not while he sat there against that boulder, talking to his Power.

One man, whose Power was that of the buffalo bull, got shot in the back, the slug flying out his chest. So he crawled on all fours into the Clearwater, fists clenched to imitate hooves, emitting the deep roar of a bull, and clotted blood flew from the wound, and he lived another thirty years. Another man had a Power that let him smell white people a mile away. His Power told him never to smoke, and to wear no clothes into battle. It showed him a fellow sitting in a blanket, back against a stump, yellow hair falling over both his shoulders, the rays of the sunlight passing over him, never hitting him. His Power told the man who saw this to bind, to his war whistle, two pinches of eagle down plucked from right above the bird's heart, because they had fluttered in something no one could see.

Wahlitits saw himself killed in a dream, four days before he died at Big Hole, face to the sky, shot through the chin, pregnant wife dead at his side. One very old man, steam rising off his wounds, rode his horse away from a skirmish, and died years later, still a prisoner. Sarplis, unwounded, opened his red flannel shirt and let a few bullets, flattened against his Power, fall to the ground. In the Bear Paw Mountains that autumn, when they surrendered, the whole landscape was letting them know whether their Power had adapted. The air thick with bullets and snowflakes, they huddled together in trenches they'd dug with knives.

Later native American tactics resembled those the Nez Percé employed, striking the enemy unexpectedly, vanishing into the countryside. Fifteen years later, fifteen hundred miles south, that fellow Geronimo also was able to disappear at will. Other Apaches said that he'd studied the Coyote Ceremony.

A story is a series of adaptations. The setting yields the characters that help, scene by scene, reveal the setting; the characters, for their part, adapt to the setting that yields them. The process so much resembles our daily experience that sometimes, as we feel a story unfold, we're struck by a curious, rather oblique observation. Doesn't all human speech, we wonder, amount to nothing more than stories—whether the remarks form a scientist's detached observations of plant or animal life, or the bedtime story that sleepy children, greedy for one more bit of emotion, insist on hearing about the days when their grandparents were children?

But like the life forms that surround us, we ourselves, collectively, amount to a story as well. We are, so to speak, the story that our stories are telling: we exist as host organisms to the remarks we pass along, to the tales we transmit about sagebrush and quail and coyotes, as well as about each other. Whether we talk about what we pray to, or how we pry nourishment from our surroundings, our stories use us up and discard us, generation by generation, adapting themselves to the changes they at once reflect and create in us. It's tricky to get just the right distance on our storytelling habits to illuminate them: think of how any tale, analyzed endlessly, begins to take on a kind of transparence. Think how the plot seems, after awhile, to be manipulating the characters, hinting that their only function has been to illustrate it.

Materializing like a ghost, like a flame of protective coloration, a mule deer buck has begun browsing our backyard willow leaves. Somehow, this afternoon, he reminds me of the kind of stories we tell and hear. He seems to appear out of nowhere, like our stories: our briefest glimpses of such things quiver, whatever it is we train on them, telescope cross hairs or literary analysis. Even when they lie gutted, feet downhill, ribcage propped open with a stick, eyes turning green—or when they sprawl roped, unskinned, to a front fender, flesh spoiling from engine heat, road dust—even at times like these, we half expect our deer to bound away. If your skinning blade so much as nicks it, the metatarsal scent gland on the hocks will foul the meat.

For no one knows how many thousands of years, hereabouts, that dark, pungent flesh has nourished human beings. Burial sites yield awls splintered from their leg bones. A paste made from their brains would soften the hide, so we could wear it. Deer hair used to stuff our saddles, even. It also stuffed those huge sofas of ours, the ones that teetered on carved wooden feet.

THREE DAYS
IN THE MEXICAN
HIGHLANDS

The road is nothing but dust and braided ruts. Dodging arroyos and boulders, we drive between *nopales* ten feet high, their trunks eighteen inches through. Now we pass under stone portals, onto the grounds of what was once a hacienda, but now serves as a ranch for raising fighting bulls. The walls are thick stone, stone the porch and patio. In the driveway we meet don Víctor, the *capataz,* or foreman, seventy years of age, his back straight and his face lined, Marlboro pack tucked in the pocket of his polo shirt. His spurs ring on the tile floor. A soft-spoken, elegant courtesy emanates from him. He introduces us to Eduardo, a young matador from Madrid who's going to test six heifers this afternoon. Don Víctor needs to know whether to breed them to the seed bulls, or send them to the slaughterhouse.

At one end of a corral, its stone walls eight feet high, six full-grown fighting bulls lounge. They're waiting to be shipped, next Sunday, to a corrida in San Luis Potosí. They're huge, shambling, gray and black with curved, fine-tipped horns and great, dark eyes. They stare at our car. They give ground grudgingly. In a group like this, they're mild mannered, don Víctor insists. Only when they're alone, as they will be in the ring, does the urge to attack surface in them. Here they're fed and herded always from trucks, or from horseback. In fact the matador who capes and kills them will be the first man they've ever seen on foot. They're so intelligent that, given a chance to improve their attack, they'd kill any matador who ever lived.

We drive to a bullring that perches high on a hillside, overlooking a lake and a mountain range. Two villages glitter in the distance, over the whitewashed wall on which don Víctor and Eduardo are unrolling thick capes, bloodstains spotting the raw pink canvas. They fit swords into the stop-sign red *muletas*, or killing capes.

Bony and quick, black as her own shadow, the first heifer bolts through the gate. She sprints across the dry grass. She and Eduardo lock into pose after pose, his back bending just enough to let her pass on one side, only to pivot, receiving her on the other. Each time he changes direction, his leather boots lift little exclamation points of dust from the earth. After twenty minutes, she's horning and pawing the dirt, nostrils flaring, confused. Eduardo climbs to the stand where we sit in the shade. Only from up close can we see he too is breathing hard, a V of sweat spreading over his shirt front. While we drink beer and make small talk, he sips a glass of water and mumbles a few remarks. Eyes narrowed, don Víctor keeps on taking notes in a huge leather-bound journal.

By sundown, the last heifer locked away, don Víctor nods to two cowboys relaxing under a *nopal*. They build a fire on the concrete steps, lay an iron sheet across the top, and start a dozen thin-sliced steaks sizzling. They put tortillas to warming at the edge.

We've spent the whole day judging the ferocity of these animals. Now we're chewing their tough, juicy flesh in the evening breeze, watching the lights of towns blink into place, miles below.

By the time the sun's up, tilting shadows and brightening tree-tops, the city of Morelia drops away. The highway's climbing. Green hills pitch and roll, dip and divide. Hours pass before we begin to see what we've come for. But now, lurching one by one, indirect as thought itself, huge monarch butterflies appear at our windshield.

With every hundred yards we gain in height, the air turns more alive, more vivid with their flight. We pass a gully spanned by a wooden bridge. The planks glow with rust-colored wings. As we look out over the countryside, it seems to shiver—like a trite landscape painting somebody's pitched onto a bonfire, the blue sky and green hills about to disappear under a million brush strokes the color of one dull flame.

Their shadows turn black on the dust that rises off our steps. (We've left our car behind by now. We scarcely noticed when we started walking.) Butterfly shadows flicker over our bodies, over our faces that drip sweat, our mouths that have started to gasp in the thin ten-thousand-foot air and the billowing dust. With an absentminded, half-reflexive nod we pay for a ticket. We agree to let some young man act as our guide. We start up the last, steepest section, part of a government preserve. Steps cut in the narrow dirt trail guide our footing. Ropes strung on either side keep us on the path.

The pines and *oyamel* trees rising out of the undergrowth stand a couple of hundred feet high. In and out of their shade, through the narrow shafts of sunlight, orange splashes blur. Behind our own breathing we can hear the light hiss of millions of wings. We step as carefully as we can over the bright dead wings underfoot. We pass a creek the surface of which is a shifting, incandescent coat of butterflies sipping water. On tree trunk and twig, even on the hand ropes either side of us, pairs of butterflies are coupling, rocking back and forth, having at each other. When our eyes accustom to the dimness at the top of the path, we notice a faint orange cast to the lowest branches, a hundred or so feet above our heads. The needles are nearly the color of evergreen boughs dead from acid rain. . . . But we realize, with a shock, that we aren't looking at needles. So many millions of butterflies cling to the boughs that they droop in great globular masses, swarming lobes of breathing, reproducing color.

They live on the nectar of these tiny red and blue blossoms, says our guide. (We'd forgotten about him entirely!) He says the butterflies mate here, and then fly north for six weeks, to Canada, to lay their eggs and die. As if waking from a deep sleep, we realize that hundreds of people surround us, up and down the trail, sweating, gasping, and staring overhead. People in fact are crowding us from behind, so we need to leave, to walk downhill to the parking lot. A blink at a time, as if we're getting released from a dream, we distinguish our fellow human beings, one from another.

On her palm, the woman beside me cups a dying butterfly like a fresh wound. Our guide tells her she can't keep it. She shows him, on its left wing, a tiny stamp she says identifies it as having come from Los Angeles. She wants to mail it to entomologists there, she says. No, says the guide, it has to stay here. She pleads. And he insists. And then he gently, gently shakes it from her hand onto the ground.

Another couple of hundred feet farther down, we leave the preserve behind, only to be surrounded by teenage boys swatting butterflies out of the air with willow switches. Each wants a tip for having guarded our car so "vandals" couldn't scratch its paint.

And then, at the very foot of the trail, we run across a heavyset woman of sixty or so with twisted legs. She's lurching uphill on a pair of aluminum crutches, step by step. With a quiet tact our guide steps in front of her, and advises her to turn back. Why? she demands. The ascent is very steep, he explains, and you'll never make it. The grin she turns on him makes us all step back. *Una apuestita, que tal?* Wanna make a little bet I won't? With a wink, the lady digs in the tips of her crutches. She starts uphill.

This country keeps bobbing up, image by image, out of what-
ever loose fluidity it is that washes us back and forth across it.
Sure, we can intuit likenesses, here and there. Certain qualities
of coherence do indeed bind our different days, one to the other.
But those qualities, such as they are, just plain don't show up
in the notes I scribble, compulsively, mornings and evenings.
As soon as the ink's dry, my sentences elude any narrative con-
struction I try to put on them. They won't resolve, even, into
detailed descriptions. The landscape's very vividness seems to
prevent my writing about it. Some angle of perception is forever
distracting me: a hummingbird, a hamburger. . . .

I came here to register, in words, the nuances and garish
contrasts of being here. But everything's too discontinuous. I
figure that this countryside, if it were itself a kind of writing,
would have to be fragments. It'd be the kind of journal that I
wind up keeping while here, repetitive but full of gaps, zealous
yet elliptical, stuttering with stubbornness, stunned at its own
lack of fluency. So maybe my pages do catch the landscape that
occasions them, at least in a clumsy, imitative way.

But not really. Because now that I think about it, if the Mexi-
can highlands were a kind of writing, they'd have to be mar-
ginal notes. They would amount to the kind of comments we
find handwritten in some used book—or one of those counter-
arguments that we discover, scrawled alongside the principal
points, running through some old volume that we've checked
out of a library: we almost can understand such quirky, periph-
eral passages, but really and truly, to follow them, we need to
refer to the printed text. The difference is, of course, that this
countryside describes an invisible text.

The landscape around us seems, frequently enough, to re-
fer beyond itself—as if it were some language that I only
half understood, purring along implying a wider, more elusive
meaning I can't quite catch. I often feel like it's signaling in

some kind of code, aiming a subtle message at me, hinting, in-sinuating: now I drowse, limp on a bench, digesting the flesh of animals bred for their stamina and their ferocity; and now I utterly lose track of where I am, even believing I'm alone, while standing in fact surrounded by people every bit as spellbound as I am by bits of existence both evanescent and endless. It's easy to understand why the Aztecs used to believe this earth and sky amounted to a complex of comments, a kind of writing which, if we could read it, would describe the thoughts of the gods.

Bulls and butterflies! That's what this place comes down to—disparate signals, incompatible emblems. It offers no interpre-tive key, no central place from which to observe it, no unquiver-ing pivot from which the different blurs resolve into figure and ground. Whichever direction we look, the focus of attention seems to lie way beyond our windshield. Wherever we stop, the countryside is all border, boundary, edge, and rim. So we keep on driving through it.

The main highway into Guanajuato follows an ancient riverbed, the bottom and sides of it lined with stones round as human heads. First we dip below ground level and then, as we enter a tunnel, those smooth granite spheres seal us off, on all sides, even above, from the light and air. Then we surface into traffic exhaust and skinny dogs.

From our hotel roof, we can see that the town lies wedged in a narrow valley two miles long, say, by maybe a mile in width. It seems casual, almost accidental, the way the brightly colored houses spill down the bare slopes in ever denser patterns, until they collide at the bottom, a splash of green and red and yel-low. Here and there, out of the seethe of traffic and pastel walls, rises the bell tower of a sixteenth-century church, the facade of an eighteenth-century government building. That low, mas-sive block-long structure dominating the downtown was the granary in which the Spaniards stored their munitions during the War of Independence. The local kid whose statue overlooks the whole valley sneaked in during a battle and torched the door, allowing the insurgents to dispatch the Spanish defenders, earning his name a place on the wall of heroes.

As we walk the streets our perspective dips and rises, fitfully. Vistas keep breaking out—between two buildings, through a window, around a corner. Long narrow alleys snake uphill, the buildings on either side so close their windowsills nearly touch. (One alley is said to be so narrow that lovers on opposite balconies can kiss.) Third-story and fourth-story curtains shiver, pigeon colored, in breezes. Height and narrowness lend a peculiar leverage to each glimpse of this city.

Even its museum, commemorating the city's history, yields a burst of oblique angles, a precarious balance of complementary thought departures. Behind thick glass, the granite skull and the clay coyote eye each other. The flower stela appears to interpret the posture of the polished goddess, her belly swollen. All of Mesoamerica seems, for a moment, caught in one smooth white stone. Three perfect breasts are growing from it.

Its museum suggests the degree to which Guanajuato has managed to adapt to the landscape that it occupies, to these hills that feel like they're riddled with hints and allusions: this is a city of discontinuous glimpses, no one of which can stand for the city itself. But a certain cohering of the senses acts almost like muscle memory, creating the shared impressions that let the locals live together, the civic common denominator that nourishes life up and down these slopes.

One museum display, for example, consists of a hundred photographic portraits of married couples, each dutifully training their eyes on the camera. Lace bodice or bleached cotton skirt, riding boot or huarache, straw sombrero or wilting corsage—embracing the conventions that disclose their sense of who they are, they eye the lens, and turn permanent. The moment we step outside the long room that houses the photos, we notice a plaque telling us that, in the War of Independence, the pink and tan slabs of the room's exterior wall served another method of stopping time, as well. They provided the backstop against which the colonial governor's firing squads squinted, at one patriot after another, flexing their trigger fingers.

Farther down the block, on a wall of the house where he was born, the furtive, preoccupied eyes of a famous muralist peer from his own self-portrait. Brass bed rail and limestone patio fountain, the furnishings from the end of the last century leave the rooms looking just the way they did when he was a boy. Right here he would've learned to walk, between skylight and floor tile.

At the start of the last century, right around the corner, above the granary's stone wall, the colonial governor ordered his troops to display, in a metal cage, the severed head of the Father of Independence. Right up there, it would've hung. The patriots would have stared and pointed. He must've looked as if, at last, he'd found a place from which he could observe the entire city.

THE REPUBLIC
OF BOYLSTON

The Cascade mountain valley I live in lies bisected by a twenty-mile railroad embankment. Pasture and hay field alike bear that raised welt of engineering. No tracks, though, and no ties. The railroad tore them out the moment it discontinued service five, or was it six, years ago. An aerial view would show the embankment running straight as a blade swipe, southeast to northwest, sagebrush arroyo to Ponderosa creek bank. At either end, it disappears into a tunnel.

The southeastern of the two tunnels lies ten miles from my front door. To get there I drive off through sagebrush, trailing a hundred-yard plume of dust. Cow pies and wild roses and blue sky mark the spot. When I try to reconstruct the thinking that drilled two thousand feet through solid rock—only to rip out, seventy years later, both the ties and the rails—a certain grim glee overcomes me. The railroad even deeded the right-of-way to the state. Sometimes I stand at the mouth of my tunnel, right at the thirty-foot lips, and shout into that dark throat. But a cave-in a couple of hundred feet back flattens the echo, every time, to a perfectly ordinary drawl.

That a man should get reduced to talking to an empty tunnel! Why, it probably makes this place where I live seem like the very edge of the earth. But I retreat to that hole in the hillside the way a fly finds a swatter handle the perfect place to meditate. I relax in the gap that dynamite pried between boulders. After all, I'm making a living, this summer, by talking literary theory with a dozen public-school English teachers.

They're sharp, and good-natured, and snap up important ideas. They read the assignments every day, but get thoroughly puzzled at a certain line of thinking: that terms like *sonnet* and *blank verse* are only decoding tools, nothing more than the strategies a reader employs to pattern his or her responses. They shrug and stare out the window, as soon as they hear the claim of one theorist—that readers who share a number of such strategies amount to an "interpretive community." Such talk baffles my friends, the teachers. Isn't the sonnet a form, after all? And if meaning resides in the readers' responses, where does that leave a teacher's authority? Back and forth, we discuss it, five mornings a week. Every other evening or so I repair to my tunnel entrance, there to sit and smoke and watch the shadows lengthen, there to consider both strategy and community.

I know the thing is a tunnel, because I remember the railroad. Indeed I've seen other tunnels, and other embankments. But lacking all familiarity with the demands of American commerce, what would I make of so much moved earth and blasted rock? Might I not sense, behind it all, some kind of religious motive? When I measured, and found the ruling grade to be four-tenths of one percent, and a hole on either end, mightn't I envision some processional, gaudy with priests and offerings? Lately a lot of careful envisioning, with the help of microfilm copies of local newspapers, has let me begin to feel what that tunnel meant to the people whose lives it changed. Hour after hour I sit, reeling back to the first six months of 1908, when the tunnel was news.

From the tenth of January, 1908, for example, I find a couple of columns headlined "Human Derelicts Illustrate Biblical Story." Many an honest hard-working man in a penniless plight, it seems, finds himself killing time in the Great Northern depot, or in the Third Street Reading Room. In the latter, we discover those who yet keep some grip on respectability, though making no effort to better their condition; while the depot waiting room, raided almost nightly by the police, collects the "dyed in the wool" hobo, tireless only in his pursuit of whiskey. Either fellow, full of hints of once-better fortunes, voice limping from "if" to "might have been," illustrates the bitter truth of our reaping as we sow. Some, in the reading room, can talk like professional men. Perched in the warmest corner, evenings, they condemn the present form of government, being themselves of a socialist leaning, and versed in political issues, most of their faces bearing the lines of the strong drink to which they attribute their downfall. Even more degraded, those at the depot have turned by preference to crime and petty thieving. Only yesterday a well-known hay man inquired of three such fellows, standing on the platform, whether they would help him for a few minutes, offering a fair price for their services. They gazed at him in amazement. They leered in his face.

And yet by January fifteenth, the spirits of the very same paper, appropriately named the *Localizer,* trill like a winter bird on a feeder: a standing order is in for ten men every day at one of the grading camps; stagecoaches go loaded daily for points on the Columbia River. The Milwaukee line is really and truly going to pass through here! Contractors report that work is further advanced than they'd planned.

January 26 brings an interview with a Mr. Jacobson, senior partner in the firm grading, drilling, and laying the rails. He glows reminiscent, over an after-dinner cigar, to tell us that he and a Mr. Lindstrom began it all by landing together in New York, "strangers in a strange land." Shipping to Iowa to work with pick and shovel on the Milwaukee line extension, in months they saved and pooled enough to buy an ancient mule and a scraper outfit. With the persistence characteristic of their nationality, they prospered till, in 1885, they bought their first railroad outfit. The current job embraces over a million cubic yards of rock. Already it employs more than five hundred men, day and night, in fourteen camps supported by twenty-three cooks and 180 head of horses.

In part, reading the *Localizer* amounts to pure escape. Most mornings by nine-thirty I slink out of the library stacks, irritated at how bland and gray those days make my own appear. In the classroom, the very next hour, it may sound like I'm reviewing Iser's notion of our anticipation and retrospection, moment by moment, while reading a text. And in one sense, I am. But meanwhile, in another corner of my mind, I'm remembering February of 1908. I'm recalling how, in a single twenty-four hours, one man was killed by dynamite, and another found a diamond: such was the energy released by moving a million cubic yards of rock. Gustaf Erickson forgot to watch for an old blast, from weeks before, one that never had gone off. His drill struck it. He got thrown seventy feet in the air, and the fall broke his neck. The same day G. N. Rice, local division manager, while walking through Johnson Canyon, picked up and brought to town the attractive stone a Seattle jeweler later ordered sent to a lapidary for examination. The *Localizer* muses, nostalgic, for five column inches: twenty-some years ago, forty miles north, a civil engineer on the Great Northern survey found a stone that he sent, when he returned to New York, to Tiffany's. They pronounced it a diamond worth nine hundred dollars.

Often enough the coming of the railroad stirs the *Localizer* to a kind of greedy hyperbole. By mid-March we learn that more acres lie open, adjacent to these new tracks, than one can find anywhere else in all of the Republic. Millions, and of the very finest land, are soon to be available, from Missouri River to Pacific Coast. Meanwhile, the paper purrs over local progress: 2,400 men are laying 2,000 feet per day of 935-pound steel rails, heavier than those of either Northern Pacific or Great Northern. What the company calls a continuous rail will minimize the sway of the cars, and eliminate the familiar click-clack. On March 19, by company calculation, the largest pile of railroad ties in all the United States lies at Murdock, or a couple of miles out of town. They number more than one hundred thousand.

The paper advances a smugly ethnic interpretation of labor. Now a crew of Italians will be replaced by Americans and Swedes, as the natives of sunny Italy are long on talk and sociability, but shy when it comes to handling rails. And now a month later, the shipping in of Italians and Bulgarians has nearly ceased: aliens are used only in work others will not perform, because a Swede or American will do in a day three times as much as the dark skinned of southern Italy and Europe. Indeed, on March 21, a grading crew of thirty men fought with shovels, picks, and fists for an hour. Blacks and Swedes took on the Italians. Later, with one man injured seriously, and the heads of several others broken, rumor had it that some fellow had hauled into camp a large quantity of whiskey.

The idle and the curious flock to the valley. On March 17 we meet Ah Dye, close to forty, the "world's only Chinese hobo," in our city paying a visit to his brethren and countrymen. A cook by profession, in logging camps and on shipboard, he has taken a turn through every state west of the Rockies, not to mention Mexico, Alaska, Honolulu, and the Philippines, spending his money over the bar, or gambling. He dresses neatly, and but for the indelible looks and manner of his people, would never be taken for a son of the "flowery kingdom." He has fallen into the meshes of the law more than once, serving time on the chain gangs of a dozen cities. Three days later, we meet Alexander Barrie. Six feet seven in his stocking feet, once a circus sideshow giant, and now wrecked from drink, he eats glass to amuse saloon loafers, chewing up any form of it whatever, wanting only a "chaser." He has a double set of teeth, and stomach and digestive organs of a peculiar character. As apparently he cannot keep from begging, the police have run him out of town.

Consider, on the other hand, the good luck of Nick Colton.

A laboring man from Kingman, Arizona, employed by the Milwaukee extension, he quit one night before the line was even finished, and hopped a lumber car on an eastbound freight. Compelled by the crew to get off at Cle Elum, he seized a brake beam and hitched a ride. Before long, the train jarred his balance, and he rode fifteen miles with one foot dragging over the ties. Taken down exhausted in this city, he suffered only a badly bruised heel. But his heavy logging boot was shredded.

Soon enough, though, other stories replaced that of the railroad. Indeed, the attention span of the *Localizer* suggests that we tired of the railroad even before it inaugurated service—seventy-five years, in fact, before it got tired of us. Maybe we started missing the dynamite and the foreigners. Maybe that nearly religious impulse to rearrange rock in angles and lines just plain wore itself out here. No Pyramid of the Sun, thank you. A hole through a mountainside and twenty miles of incline register our otherworldliness. Even by March 2, John Jackson had lost his enthusiasm. After lighting a four-foot fuse, at a site a few miles outside Easton, about 8:30 A.M., rather than running he stood on a nearby rock ledge, ignoring the pleas of his coworkers. He was thrown twenty feet in the air, and took ten minutes to die. A foreman contends it was suicide. Jackson had gone on a protracted spree, he says, and arrived at work quite despondent.

And then one day, before I expect it really, the last class meeting is over. The teachers have gone. They do leave behind them, though, the usual feeling that I've forgotten to tell them something. Then I sense what it is. Suddenly I know why I've spent my mornings in the library, my evenings in the sagebrush. My own behavior was trying to tell me something: I should have compared the act of reading with that of passing through a tunnel. I should've led the teachers to see that no isolated moment of either act can represent, without distortion, the durational flow from which we abstract it. We confirm, at the moment the last rhyme takes hold, that the poem is a sonnet, but only then. So a lot of literary vocabulary the teachers have mastered refers to no more than one moment in a process, the moment when we succeed in identifying which of a given number of forms is being exploited. Such terms are helpful, sometimes. But at their worst, they leave the poems seeming more a puzzle than a bit of passionate speech. The poem seems to exist only to be "solved" by English teachers such as my friends and me.

My hours studying that tunnel tell me something else as well. They suggest that, from any artifact, whether it's a tunnel or a text, we can infer a lot about the people for whom it's intended. Because the embankment crosses our valley without swerving, for example, we can infer it must have had priority over all that lay originally in its way. From the exactitude of its gradient, we can infer the value the railroad put on saving fuel. In a similar way, I wish I'd told those teachers, a text can characterize for us the audience for which it is written.

Take for example you yourself, the person reading these pages. I can be sure you know a certain amount about the American West. Only through your preexisting sense of this town's isolation, eighty years ago, could these paragraphs convey to you our excitement at the railroad's approach. You probably know that, during the late 1860s, a certain William Cody contracted to provide meat for railroad workers. You may even know that, by the nineties, half a world away, the petty criminals of Paris, the enforcers, the cutpurses, called themselves Apaches. Almost surely you know that what the world considers the American West lasted for only that pair of decades.

I think my own thought patterns this summer resemble, for sheer compulsion, the building of that tunnel and embankment. Suppose, for a moment, that we could ask him. What motives would Mr. Jacobson cite to justify all that manpower and expense? Indeed, what would one of his laborers say? Well, either might have muttered truisms about "progress." But you and I, eighty years removed, feel tempted to believe that they had other motives as well. We can suspect they wanted to control the landscape, to neutralize both the size and the contour of it, and that "progress" provided a convenient excuse. We don't know that for sure. But we can suspect.

By the same token, someone distant enough might see, more

clearly than you and I, not only my motives for writing these pages but, as well, your own for reading them. And to what motives would such a person attribute this exchange between us? That person might suggest that you and I, here in these pages, constitute a community rather like the one maintained, even now, by the former residents of Boylston.

Boylston? Once it was the last stop the train made on this side of my tunnel, about a quarter-mile from the entrance. Now, you might call it a ghost town. At its peak population, maybe a hundred people lived in the sagebrush out there. It had a hotel, and a schoolhouse even, right beside the tracks. A few years ago, when I first saw it, two concrete foundations marked where the school and the hotel must have stood. But now there's only bare dirt.

Seven big locust and catalpa trees, shoulder to shoulder south of the embankment, cast their shade on seven squares of earth packed down, each the size of a house floor. A friend can remember, from twenty-five years ago, a general store and a huge water barrel. But when the wind blows through Boylston, anymore, there's not a single hinge left to squeak. Still, simply in agreeing it was once a railroad town, we make ourselves honorary citizens of the place.

Let us, you and I, consider ourselves an interpretive community. A rusty spike, a wild rosebush—out of such signals, wielding the name Boylston as a decoding tool, we build the sympathies we respond to. Notice, for example, that each house foundation was laid out so as to train the evening breeze on the front door. Notice how thick the sagebrush grows all around where the houses stood. Men and women who wanted to flirt, or children playing hide and seek, people who needed to be alone could walk off in any direction they wanted.

TOMBS

Again and again the bus driver wipes his steering wheel with a rag. Centered above the windshield hangs a crucifix of bronze, sunlight through the trees glittering off the Lord's muscle definition. The pink beads and thin chain of a rosary hang wrapped around him. Tucked into the visor, directly above the driver's gaze, is a color photo of a young woman wearing only a man's shirt, open at the front. She's feigning disinterest in the camera, looking instead at a book she holds in her right hand. She's seated. Her legs are spread, and her left hand dangles a handkerchief over her crotch. The Lord and the Lady, between them, seem to exert a curious balance. They wring a certain equilibrium out of whatever image fills the windshield. Her nipples are almost exactly the same pink as the rosary beads that coil around him.

Well, not exactly. Her nipples are really more nearly the rusty red of the furrows and roof tiles gliding through the windshield. The driver takes the rag to the dashboard, the windshield, the steering wheel again. He passes on curves, and floors it on flat land. At an intersection a drunk, slouching in and out of each stride, waves off the driver's warning honk, weaving across the road, making us wait. Like a dog, a billy goat scratches one ear with a hind foot, a pair of grapefruit-size testicles dangling under him. Disposable diapers and fruit rinds fill the culverts. Over hill after hill our pair of effigies seems to lead us onward. Sky reaches through the windshield, wide, blue, endless. The Lady continues pursing her lips at her book. And the Lord just keeps on dying. Even though the glitter of light on his ribcage gives the illusion that he's breathing.

In a pickup outside a bus depot, my godson and his brother wait to drive me to the house of my compadre. Seventeen and eighteen, full of a goosey, wisecracking energy, they accuse each other of driving like *indios*. With great disdain they allow as how all Mexican towns are alike: cars parked on the sidewalk, people walking in the street. Like all my compadre's kids, they've grown about six inches since I last saw them. Suddenly now, at the front door, tall, slender young strangers, wearing the faces of children I remember from five years ago, surround me with handshakes and hugs, wondering how I've been. My compadre and I sit up till four A.M., remembering the girls we used to date, the tequila we drank, the places we hitchhiked. I fall asleep with the leaves of an avocado tree brushing the window.

I haven't seen my buddy Pilar in five years. But the next afternoon, when he rolls down the street in a wheelchair, legs under a blanket, grunting a little with every push he exerts, I'm astounded. He invites me over for lunch, and explains that when a couple of gunmen robbed his gas station, they shot him in the spine. For the last five months he's had no feeling below the waist. Since the business was going to hell without him, he's closed it, and now waits for a buyer. We chew one tortilla after another, dipping them in hominy soup, washing it all down with shots of *charanda*. Since the doctors have told him he'll never walk again, he says his recovery plans mainly involve regaining control of his bowels and bladder. The humiliation of needing help on the toilet has taught him what's important, he announces with a grin.

I listen hard to his voice, and study his face. He seems to be training a kind of detached, plate-glass scrutiny on himself. It's as if he'd found his entire past locked in a museum case, and now walked around it, studying each angle, as if he were going to have to leave it, and wanted to remember every detail. Right now, for example, he's recalling the different times he and his uncle sneaked across the border to work wet in Texas, or California, picking or hoeing or irrigating. Once when the border patrol caught them, they spent fifteen days in jail. After awhile, with a pair of dice he found under a bunk, he was cleaning out the other prisoners. That time, he says with a giggle, he took more money home from the United States than ever before.

Above a blue lake, below a blue sky, five burros graze at the foot of a platform stretching an eighth of a mile. Joined by the long, narrow base out of which they protrude, five semicircular stone structures—or *yácatas*—lie on top of the platform. They exist in varying stages of repair: on the easternmost structure, the flat interior stones have been set back in place, then covered with square and oblong finishing stones, the surfaces of the latter still bearing faint carvings and pigment stains. The middle structure slumps into rubble, the dirt and spherical rocks that fill it spilling onto the ground.

The rubble represents, the caretaker tells me, the way the Spaniards left nearly all of this ceremonial center. They tore it down, first, in search of the gold ornaments that adorned the dead kings buried beneath it. Later they came here to get building materials. The reconstructions represent archaeologists' best guess about how the stones used to fit together. From where we sit, at the base of the second *yácata,* the whole platform leads the eye out over the red-tile roofs of the town below it, out to the lake and then to a shaggy line of volcanic mountains, and the sky. A dog keeps barking in the distance. Wind makes a steady hiss in the cedar boughs all around us.

Each finishing stone is about the length of my forearm, cut from a pitted volcanic material. A kind of white mortar binds them in place. The carvings are low relief, mainly of a concentric-circle motif, representing the sun. The pigment is hard to tell from the lichen that seems to spring out everywhere, blue, white, green, yellow even. A single maguey grows in the rubble, as well as a few tiny red flowers. Between the two states of repair, the *yácata* and the rubble mound, we find a deep pit in the shape of a T. Some hundred feet by seventy-five, and fifteen to thirty feet deep, it apparently held the severed heads of sacrifice victims. Their last view would have been of this blue, wide lake. Then an obsidian blade split their chests apart.

Southeast of the platform, we find the site of other sacrifices: a series of waist-high stone walls, and the stone-lined drainage ditch, a foot deep, that carried blood downhill to the lake. Today nobody knows what use the walls had. For us, they act like a maze, a baffle to any effort we make to imagine how it felt to live here above this lake, below this sky. The caretaker walks my wife and me out to the parking lot. As kids follow, wanting to sell us wheat stalks woven into ancient fertility figures, the stone walls soak up sunlight. Right here, five hundred years ago, people like us cut out each other's hearts.

And then other people like us tore down these walls for the stone that was in them. To see what use the Spaniards made of all that carved volcanic building material, my wife and I walk downhill a quarter-mile. We enter a long, bright atrium landscaped with hundred-foot cedars and concrete benches. We find here and there, each protected by a concrete base, a few dozen olive trees that the Spaniards brought in the mid-1500s. Some flourish, their leaves rippling above gnarled, knobby trunks ten feet thick. Others, long dead, twist the bare silver wood of their branches against the sky.

We find, at the end of the atrium, the open-air chapel in which the first shy, suspicious Indians huddled to hear a few strange, black-robed men speaking broken Purépecha. To the left of it lies a convent. When the tall door creaks open, we stand in a sixteenth-century courtyard, blinking at the poinsettia plant. As our eyes accustom to the light, we notice a familiar shape to the blocks of stone from which the walls and pillars are constructed. Sure enough, as we look closer, concentric circles come into focus. A sun sign engraved on the walls of a nunnery! With stone they pried from an altar built to hold shuddering human hearts, the Spaniards reared a refuge for the chaste brides of Christ.

The last five centuries, of course, have muted such garish clashes of faith. Most of what we see, here and now, amounts to no more than the earthly remains of some world view or other. These stones for example are mainly old, no matter what faith they happen to serve at the moment. Though the plaster walls all around us do bear many original frescoes. Their human figures hover, like spectral presences, the brush strokes barely clinging to the plaster.

The Queen of Heaven is vanishing into the white blur left by whatever weather it is that dissolves her, year after year. And yet, the maguey plant at her feet looks nearly as green as the one that grows, down the road, on the sacrificial platform. The wise men and the child they adore flake and peel, equally, although the burro behind them retains the same color as those that graze at the platform's foot. Here a tricornered hat, and a lace cuff, peek out of the vagueness time projects on these walls. There we can see a tonsure and a sandal. The figure of a man, faded to the rusty red of furrows and roof tiles, receives extreme unction from a priest of the same color.

For several miles before we can see it, we can hear the ocean hissing, grunting, and collapsing on sand and weeds. It breaks into view between the scraggly desert shrubs, beyond the knolls that hide it, then reveal it. It never does look the way I remember it. No matter from what angle I approach, or how many years since I've seen it, I never really believe it's the same body of water I knew before, not even now, while the surf numbs my feet the way it always did. The light plays its usual tricks, dimming, brightening. It's while I'm standing here, on the west rim of the continent, looking west, that I realize I'm about to pass the first anniversary of my father's death.

He wasn't ready to die. But everything hurt so bad, after that last round of chemotherapy, that he must have felt that any change would have to be an improvement. In our last phone conversation, I kept on begging him to try harder. But he didn't care, now, what it was I wanted. There kept edging into his voice the same remote, throaty whisper I hear in front of me today, where the water slides back and forth, and the hard, tanned American students on vacation eye each other. From here, where I sit taking notes, I hear them talking about college courses, and summer jobs. All of them seem to come from Wisconsin, Minnesota, Michigan, states the newspapers say are full of snow. A girl in cutoffs says to a boy in cutoffs that she hates the thought of having to take another writing course. As I look at her, and keep on writing, I suddenly sense the way I must look to her, a grumpy, middle-aged man, alone, scribbling in a notebook. When I meet her eyes, we both giggle, and I walk off to climb the hotel steps, to find my wife sitting up from a nap, yawning, wondering where I've been.

On the way in from the airport, we kept passing cardboard and corrugated-metal shacks, huddled beside the highway, behind a barbed-wire fence. They represent another kind of drawing power, another kind of attraction that this beach exerts on people. From Bemidji it draws the weight-lifting business-administration major, as well as the anorexic fashion-design major from Flint. But it also draws, from this side of the border, country people no longer able to make a living farming outside towns named El Venado and Platanares. They climb down off rickety second-class buses and nail together, at the edge of town, huts made of scrap material. Then they set to work on the fringe of the tourist industry mopping floors, or washing dishes. So the beach brings together, if only for this moment in history, the campesino and the college student—two kinds of people who, otherwise, never could have imagined each other's existence. Of course the beach has also brought me here to write about them, to watch whatever they do to each other turn into history.

My father died on the first day of spring. It's taken me a year to realize it, though. Saying goodbye to the rigid features under that makeup, and then to the metal casket waxed and buffed bright as a car fender, and then to the windy sunlight on those Illinois clay clods, and that slot in the ground, I was too busy receding into my own distance to notice the season. But now that those days have turned into history—if only into a year's worth of it—I begin to respond to the place his death assumes in some yearly cycle, to certain qualities of air, as well as those of light, that always are going to remind me of the day I buried him.

By now it must be thawing again, releasing its yearly smells, that Midwest dirt these children have fled to acquire the tans they flex and stretch. They whistle at a frowning waiter to order *un sanduicho de jamo y un biro*. They thumb through a phrase book, explaining to the dumbfounded maid why they thought they ought to keep the hotel's towel. Half a continent north of here, miles of willow bark brighten, and bud out. Meanwhile not only these children, but also the poor who serve them, as well as my father and I, are turning into history.

Oaxaca *mezcal* and Veracruz cigar, I'm drenching my tongue in the local, the specific, the tang that different kinds of dirt impart. After a lunch of what the waiter calls Cat Soup, my wife has gone shopping. Me, I'm slouched on the central plaza, eye-ing the cathedral in which, a century and a half ago, Benito Juárez renounced his priesthood studies. Fair-skinned tourists keep on milling back and forth, quickening the air with syl-lables of French, German, English. In one corner of the plaza, a Zapotec woman in polyester slacks preaches to a crowd of twenty pigeons. Nothing has changed in the sixteen years since I last sat at this table. A pigeon perches on the tablecloth and observes me. Time stops and starts, leaps ahead and halts. It seems to pounce, to isolate a glimpse, or a smell, or a word.

A quarter-mile of used clothing spread on plastic sheets, and the canvas roped overhead against the sun, signal the start of the Saturday market, out at one edge of town. A legless man presides over five carefully piled mounds of jalapeños, each no more than a single handful. Wrapped in straw sleeping mats, bunches of flowers thick as human torsos twitch on the dolly of the kid who transports them. First a smell of fish, and then one of citrus, gets absorbed in a vague, wet-dog odor. Tubs of black beans and pumpkin seeds, of rice and of garbanzos, cast a thick shadow in which a drunk sprawls asleep, scratching his balls, while shoppers step over him. Zapotec women stroll by in long cotton skirts, their rebozos wrapped around their heads. Two of them pause, mid-aisle, to argue the durability of the big, empty pots they carry. The aisle's so narrow they stop traffic fifty feet in each direction, the lilt and drift of their voices punc-tuating each hollow boom their palms make on clay swollen like a belly.

By the time a full moon floats above the Refresquería Bum Bum, the central plaza wiggles with activity. Artisans perch on a curb, hawking earrings. Mothers dandle infants, and boys slide one protective arm around the waists of girls. The yel-low light falling out of a street lamp slides across the surface of the fountain's water, splintering where a little girl plays at drowning water bugs. The variety all around me multiplies by the minute. It becomes a stubborn, irreducible individuality, a bristling difference of stride and posture and tone of voice in each of those going past, as if the tan soil under us held powers of invention so great, so inexhaustible, I could bear to look only in glimpses. I have to keep peeking at the moon: a big white disk floating in the sky above the Government Palace, it slows the rate of change, the click of heels on lava stone, the shadows limping over shrubs.

Every day, stories float from mouth to mouth, and page to page. Like transparent parentheses, they attach to different objects, isolating them awhile from the flow of change that sweeps over park bench and pyramid alike. Nobody cares whether the stories are true. Or I don't care, anyhow. It satisfies me to learn that the *juaristas* stabled their horses under the gold-leaf ceilings of one of these chapels. I feel better remembering how—at some Mexican intersection—angry crowds disinterred the amputated leg of Santa Anna: they dug it up, from deep in its own mausoleum, and dragged it through the streets. Bits of news like these keep me scribbling away, half the night, in a second-floor hotel room. It's almost dawn when I turn the night light out, and get to sleep. A couple of hours later when I'm yawning, rubbing my eyes as my wife and I walk through the lobby, the desk clerk whispers to me that D. H. Lawrence stayed in the room down the hall.

All afternoon the road to the ruin switches back again and again, the city shrinking, all around us, to tin shacks and tree line. Dry stalks cling to the horizon. And then we're sitting among the carved rubble, the piled-up slabs, the low-relief human figures we came to see. From the highest pyramid, a breeze slips across ten miles of valley into our faces. Arranged around a central courtyard, smaller platforms of tan stone raise their right angles, their corners and stairs and doorways, out of the tan dirt. The courtyard is flat, trampled grass broken by smaller platforms and, in the middle, what may have been a pyramid for sacrifices. Butterflies plunge and soar through the vista. On the ground level, where a doorway beckons, we step between stones carved with dying human figures, into a passageway ten degrees cooler than the outdoors.

These tombs were built to stop time. Around each of the skeletons lie bowls and vases for nourishment. A gold ring gleams from a finger bone. The walls crawl with colors and shapes, with headdresses and gestures, all pinned under a hundred feet of stone. But a certain kind of thinking raised these walls, and painted them. And the same kind of thinking, two millennia later, has brought us here to stare. Because neither we nor these dead ever have managed to dodge a certain uneasy kind of awe, a vague dread of death that plays at the edge of the mind, this afternoon, just the way it did two thousand years ago. Like the dead, after all, we know the local dirt is so inventive, so capable of yielding forms of life we can't imagine, we do whatever we can to lessen the flow of change all around us.

To help stabilize our lives, to extend ourselves over time, we're visiting a few scattered bones. We even try to memorize the contortions and grimaces cut in stone all about them. We very much need to know which of all our changeable, flickering feelings it was that these dead shared. And then something remarkable happens. Time itself seems to stop. We suddenly can feel the dead counting on us, at least on our wanting to know which of these feelings it was that they shared. We feel how much they keep on needing people like us to stare at them, and nod our heads, and walk out into the sunlight.

By now I'm packing and slamming our suitcases shut, the tops of my feet a raw red, sunburned from climbing pyramid stairs in sandals. My wife keeps giggling, calling me Cuauhté-moc, after the last Aztec prince, that fellow the Spaniards strung up, and under whose feet they built a bonfire to make him tell where the gold was hidden.

On the way back from the tombs, hours ago, we walked around a huge cedar, sixty meters in circumference, two thousand years old. Now we're measuring backward in time, to make its age real to ourselves: even on the day when a few ragged, lice-ridden nomads—already proclaiming themselves the Aztec Empire—took it in mind to found a city, even then that tree was more than a thousand years old. It turned out that they settled on a spot no one else wanted, right where they found an eagle, perched on a prickly pear, eating a rattler. Three hundred years later, Cortés would find their city bigger, cleaner, and brighter than any in Europe. He fled, when he destroyed it, with so much gold that the bridges splintered under his cart wheels.

The first thing in the morning, just as they've done for weeks now, cathedral bells are groaning and tinkling their way into my sleep. In Morelia and Guanajuato, Guadalajara and Oaxaca, their devout hullabaloo's been attacking whatever window I snore behind. They seem like homely, pious widows and spinsters, early risers, drab of dress, prim of hairdo, utterly selfless in their praise and punctuality. Slipping out this morning to buy a newspaper, I pause on the sidewalk to drop another couple of coins in a beggar's hat. He's been standing for three days now on one side of the *zócalo,* his harmonica whining the same tune, his eyes closed, beside him his wife and a daughter maybe ten years old. My coins jingle into the sweat-stained straw fedora his wife props on one knee, squatting, squinting at the horizon, jaw working a bit of gum. Like that business about the bells, it amounts to another way my days keep knitting together, this habit of handing a stranger a bit of metal stamped with an Aztec eagle.

Back up in the room, when I peek under the bed, I inhale the same musty, mildewed odor that clung to the tombs we crawled into. But already I'm getting impatient. Our plane leaves in an hour. But the space under our bed is dark. So I wait till I can see whether we've left anything behind. And we haven't. Under the base of the night light, we slip a ten-thousand-peso note for the maid. We close the door.

BURNING WHAT
WE WEAVE

These mid-November weeks drain the last inches of color from the landscape. The Cascade mountain valley I live in slips below the fog or cloud cover that is going to shroud it for most of the next four months. Every once in awhile, the gloom lifts, the light comes back. But mainly we shiver over mugs of soup or coffee, while the damp pours down all around us, alternating back and forth, a snow, a drizzly rain.

People I've known for twenty years suddenly seem foolish, grotesque, intolerable. My feelings turn as stiff as the knapweed stalks gnarled in my front yard. My workday feels monotonous as those boot prints out there, freezing and thawing and freezing, marching in place up and down a few degrees of Fahrenheit, marking time. When the ground thaws it shrugs and heaves, baring rocks that glaciers have strewn either side of the creek, all the way to the river. Every spring, a few more of them peek through the thin soil, spherical as skulls, cautious, deferential.

Every fall about this time I start to feel plain terrible. Right after waking every morning, I need to sit under bright light for half an hour or so. My doctor tells me that the photons inhibit the brain's release of a certain hormone, that if I want to feel better I simply have to put in my time each morning. And he must be right. Little by little, even as I yawn and stretch, everyone I know gets more interesting. Feelings sprout all over me. I can see one green creep into the sagebrush, then another into the willow leaves, a third into the grass.

The light I sit under amounts to a way of controlling the season's effect on my feelings. My own squinting and blinking leave me feeling a lot less hopeless. But it's an inconstant companion, this gloom of mine, one every bit as fickle as the fog and overcast sky that bring it on. Sometimes all on its own my attitude will lighten up. Yesterday morning, for example, I woke too late to use my light. But driving into town in a hurry, we saw a coyote slipping across a pasture. And I felt a big burst of brightness go off in the back of my mind. Here he came loping all skinny and scruffy out of a patch of sagebrush, to cross the road in front of our fender and disappear into the cottonwoods lining the creek. He wore that sly grin they get when they run. He didn't care that he was exposed, crossing open ground. He was in no particular hurry. And a kind of otherworldly glee seized me. I wanted to leap from the car, and invent dance steps, and sing songs I'd never heard.

But I can't count on a coyote appearing every time my life feels pointless. No, I need the right tools—a big bright light, and a book, and a lot of patience—because fighting off depression is plain hard work. The 150-watt bulb I sit under was designed for growing plants; but I've got it screwed into an aluminum shade, one that clamps to the bookshelf two feet above my chair. So half an hour of imitation sunlight, at point-blank range, keeps the Columbia Plateau winter livable. Every morning I can feel my responses open like petals. The odor of coffee deepens, a breath at a time. Thread by thread, the carpet emits a mellower hue. The voice coming off the page I read begins to reach a wider range of tones, funnier, sadder, wiser, more foolish even.

My depression feels like some kind of test the landscape I

live in keeps on giving me. I have to be willing to crouch for awhile under the light, certain that I'll never feel better, before I can expect to feel better. I have to read whatever page I put before myself, ignoring all the disgust that brims over, my own revulsion at myself, as well as at whatever I'm reading about. Sitting here amounts to no more than a kind of busy work. Sometimes I think about the Abbot Paul, an ascetic monk who contended with depression, circa A.D. 400, in the Egyptian desert. Living seven days' walk from the nearest town, he spent his time gathering palm leaves, and weaving various articles from them, baskets and floor mats and the like. At the end of a whole year of weaving, when his cave stood full of his handiwork, he'd drag it all outside, and torch everything he'd done. The value of his work, he knew, lay in its power to keep his despair at arm's length. . . . Morning after morning, I grit my teeth. I need a light bulb bright as the abbot's bonfire.

It used to be about this time of year that the first people to live here would begin telling Coyote stories. Because the stories brought on change, those people always claimed they waited until the weather couldn't get any worse. By the time anthropologists got around to asking various informants, no one knew why it was that the stories guaranteed change. I figure it was because Coyote himself, the way the stories portray him, amounted to the primary agent of change hereabouts, in the landscape as well as in human living conditions. After all, he created the landforms I see out my window every morning. Though his creations did come about by accident. In most of the stories, he's wandering back and forth in an era when Animal People flourished. Native America loved to focus on the time that human beings—what Coyote and his contemporaries called the Real People—were just at the point of taking up residence here on the earth, forever susceptible to influence, to precedent.

The adventures of Coyote are endless. Lots of mornings I train my grow light on him, episode by episode, clenching myself into my chair, waiting to feel more like myself. The books that

I read about him yield a perspective at once broad and shallow, different I'm sure from anything people enjoyed a couple of centuries ago. By flipping a few pages I drop down from sagebrush highlands to the banks of the Columbia, hearing along the way a range of stories that no single person ever heard, or not in these versions anyway. I may not recognize all the plant and animal life. And I certainly don't know the languages. But my view of Coyote's adventures can't be beat for panorama. I watch him travel through scores of cultures, innumerable language groups, from people who spear fish to people who stalk buffalo. He slinks through fiercely different kinds of lives, those who cling to a daily existence nourished by roots and mice, those who every year give away tons of food and furs.

Most of the ways people live derive from some whim of his, some bit of impatience, some momentary anger or jealousy. We die for example because he couldn't keep his paws off his wife: he was returning her from the dead, and she was almost back here among the living, but he violated the rules and pounced on her, obligating people ever afterward to die. And yet, because he was generous enough to show us how to bind it, we can sling a bundle of firewood over one shoulder. The impact of his body dug Crater Lake when, lusting after a certain star, then following her, he dropped out of the sky. The cultural and biological elements of our lives, not to mention the features of the landscape that we inhabit—the substance of human life, really, owes to his personality.

Often, though, I think that his main concern is with keeping busy. He always seems about one task ahead of a deep depression. He's a little too quick with his tears or his laughter, too ready to fly into some rage (only then to forget what it was that he got angry about), a little too brash, or too cowardly, and always too quick to whip out that hyperactive penis of his. Even when he's playing the role of benefactor to human beings, he seems distracted, in a hurry, needing to be somewhere else. He made the valley I live in, I'm convinced, even the cloud cover that leaves me huddled under this light bulb, in order

to keep his mind off his troubles. Once in awhile I stare out
my window at canyons and ridges—at shapes considered his
handiwork for most of however many centuries people have
lived among them. The contours before long begin to take on
that unsteady, provisional glitter that must have gathered about
the baskets and mats the Abbot Paul set before his cave, once
a year. At such a moment I figure that the horizon really is a
by-product, a side effect of some vow to survive.

My feelings peek over an inner horizon, every morning. The
hormone that recedes before my bulb is called melatonin, a
name derived from the Greek word for *dark*. One by one my
emotions slink into view, sheepish, exposed against the back-
drop of my anticipation. Of course a skeptic would say that all
this business with the light bulb is pure ritual, that I feel better
only because I believe I will. But so what? I remind myself of
my friends the Huicholes—those Mexican Indians who hunt
peyote, as they say, "to find our lives." In order to feel better,
they say, they need to sit all night in the desert, weeping like
coyotes for their sins, burning bits of string in which they've tied
a knot for each of their love affairs, each of their attachments
to the world they've left behind. By the time the sun comes
up they're stalking their cactus, those little sagebrush-colored
asterisks on the desert floor, squinting, calling them *deer*. They
swear peyote appears only to people ready to see it. They hunt
it in San Luis Potosí, in a valley shaped like this one. Kneeling
there, years ago, I dug one out with my office key.

My Huicholito friends and I inhabit different ends of the same
stretch of mountains. The same mood swings amble back and
forth across our roads. Their desert plant pops up wild along-
side railroad tracks, or beside the telephone poles at the edge
of little towns. The filaments that throw my life in relief can
get their current from any one of this country's five thousand
hydroelectric dams, all of which are forever silting up, forever
in need of dredging to keep from becoming nothing more than
huge waterfalls. Before another thousand years have elapsed,
that massive concrete is going to look every bit as religious as

all those pyramids and ball courts that got built, south of here, to keep despair at arm's length.

As the light beats down on my page I wonder what Coyote, the creator, has to do with the scavenger that crossed the road in front of us yesterday morning. I think the mythic character is to the animal exactly what the light bulb over my head is to the sun: even while we're looking at them, natural forces become conventions of thought.

That's how they wind up turning our thought into a kind of natural force. Whatever we think about, we feel our own identity vanish before our eyes. Whoever we are, if we live here long enough we resemble Abbot Paul, training the mind on matters other than its own survival. Even though some of us, like my buddy Jake, do get distracted. A rodeo bronc rider six feet five inches tall, the m.c. of Elk Club Amateur Hour and Lookalike Night, Jake would solemnly promise to fight you or fuck you or sing you a ditty, and laugh, and pull that handlebar black mustache.

I went with him once to explore an abandoned farmhouse. He eased open the front door, and headed straight for the bathroom. He flipped open the medicine cabinet, palming and gulping the contents of a couple of prescription bottles. I wondered out loud what was in them. I'll let you know, Jake smiled, in ten or fifteen minutes. Another time he totaled the brand-new car of a girl he'd been living with. I came to in a corn field, he said in a mournful tone. I hitched into town and phoned her up collect. Told her to keep my clothes. We was through.

Jake never learned to distract himself with busy work. In the stories people tell about him, he seems forever in a frenzy, as if he'd gone numb all over, as if thrashing around would restore his ability to feel. His death, three winters ago, surprised no one. Drunk in a roadhouse parking lot in Idaho, he reached into some woman's car, right through the passenger window. Apparently he knew her. Anyhow, she swore that, when she accelerated, his arm got caught. Eleven miles of freeway later, after the highway patrol pulled her over, there was only the right arm of him left, and a head and torso. But a lot of us think now that maybe his arm never did get caught. We figure that maybe his grip was just that strong.

Natural forces, conventions of thought, whatever they are they keep coming back. They keep us alive awhile, till one of them carries us off, limp as a rabbit between a coyote's jaws. That's what happened to Jake. Maybe he just ran out of luck. Or maybe, one of those times he forgot to ignore his own despair, the landscape ate him up. He sure didn't survive the contours that power my light bulb.

The sun evaporates water and melts snow, filling creeks that run downhill and into rivers that yield the power that makes my filaments glow. However indirect the route the sun takes to reproduce itself, it lets me see the range of colors the absence of sunlight has dimmed. Over a route just as indirect, in and out of skinny, scruffy individuals' behavior, Coyote also reproduces himself. That's how he restores a range of feelings to us.

No one has ever succeeded in domesticating the coyote. Sometimes they mate with dogs, but the offspring never can be trained or trusted. Some ethologists argue the coyote amounts to an older, less specialized canine form, one from which both wolf and dog descended. I can believe it. After all, the character of Coyote shows how people manage to inhabit these gullies and draws, this land that simply won't become imagination's pet. In order to survive, he has to be willing to give up all permanence. People the length of this whole mountain range told stories about the same moody creator, in hundreds of different languages, thousands of different names for him, his only constant a shifty personality: treacherous and kind, foolish and tragic, silly and sad. A lot of mornings, crouched in my beam of light, I have to giggle out the window at all those different feelings, up and down the bare basalt, switching their stories on and off, looking around and grinning.

BORDERS

With the signing in 1847 of the Treaty of Guadalupe Hidalgo, the Rio Grande became the border between Texas and Mexico. And citizens of the town of Laredo turned into Texans. Shortly thereafter, one hundred or so families dismantled their houses, dug up their dead, and moved across the river, thus regaining the Mexican citizenship that the treaty had cost them.

I've always admired their decisiveness. Even from a vantage point a century and a half removed in time, I almost can see their spades prying the dead from dry ground, only to tuck them back in ground equally dry, a mile or so to the south. I can see them driving their pigs and skinny cows across the river. Rolling hills of pale dirt and chaparral, the river's twin banks would've resembled each other far more, then, than they do now. But they didn't seem alike to those Laredans. No, to them a difference far deeper than the river divided the two countries, a difference which in time became pronounced enough for all the world to see.

I myself came first to the Rio Grande Valley at age twenty-three, newly out of graduate school, to teach courses in composition and literature to freshmen in El Paso. With all the energy of a kid let out of class, I dedicated my evenings and weekends to prowling the environs. The river that ran beside El Paso divided it from what local boosters loved to call its "sister city," Cd. Juárez, Chihuahua. And sisters the two towns may have been. They certainly did share a painful, awkward resemblance. The aluminum and glass of high-rise, commercial El Paso seemed an ugly mockery of Juárez's broken sidewalks and muddy alleys. Whining for dimes on the international bridge, the ragged kids just south of the midpoint seemed a reductionist, half-satiric version of the brokers and lawyers in summer-weight suits who ambled through El Paso's central plaza. Like the tines of a fork, the two sides of the river pinned my attention in place. All that poverty and wealth, the Mexican and Anglo world views the river spliced together—the whole landscape seemed to consist of counterparts precariously balanced, of contraries calculated to leave no middle ground. And even today, after having lived for the intervening quarter-century in the Pacific Northwest of the United States, as well as in central Mexico, I've never gotten beyond those first impressions. A certain binary brusqueness, a type of garish twinning seems to characterize my briefest thought of the border, let alone my dimmest memory of it.

The Rio Grande Valley amounts, today, to an area unique in international relations. Nowhere else in the world do want and affluence eye one another in quite so intense a form, held apart by nothing more than a few feet of water. Yet neither troops nor watchtowers guard, throughout most of its miles, that ambience the river creates, an eerie region of oppositions so vivid and unexpected that visitors from either country's interior reel, often as not, from a kind of cultural whiplash.

This past summer my wife and I decided to visit the border. Often we'd flown above it, on the way to and from Guadalajara. But this time we meant to explore a representative length of it. This was August, after all. We each had a month off from school, and she knew nothing but what I'd told her about that edge of the country. So one day we pack a couple of bags and drive southeast, vowing to observe for a while the contradictions of life along the Río Grande, or along the Río Bravo, its very name depending on whether observers stand to the north of the river, or south.

Before long, El Paso quivers onto our windshield like a mirage we're about to enter. Its own Sun Belt prosperity nudges the city north, acre by acre, advancing over cuesta and arroyo, the dry rocky dirt bristling with yucca and ocotillo, barrel cactus and prickly pear and cholla. We almost can feel rattlesnake and coyote giving ground, before bank branch and shopping center and condominium. Aluminum and brick and steel climb skyward in all directions. Windows tinted against the sun reflect the observer's gaze every which way, lending a dim anonymity to those who, behind them, pursue careers with the various corporations and chains represented up and down the length of Mesa Street. From desert edge to downtown plaza, impersonality and newness fight for our every glance. Even the fast-food restaurant that serves us lunch has opened only the week before. (Plucking tinfoil from microwaved enchiladas, we wonder how long it will last.) Waitress and gas-pump attendant tell us to have a nice day. Trained to exude a standardized pleasantness, they glance at our check or credit card, and proceed on a first-name basis. And yet, the nearer we approach the downtown and its river, the more all this bland impermanence loosens its grip on the skyline. The Safeways give way to corner grocery stores with *La Esperanza* or *La Reina* lettered in peeling script on plate glass. Landscaped office complexes offering underground parking become brick apartment buildings, laundry fluttering over their fire escapes. Corporate anonymity yields, block by block, to a poverty utterly particular, unchangeable as a last name.

Across the river in Juárez rise the same drab buildings and store fronts that I remember, more sun bleached now, a sign changed here and there. Angling in and out of traffic, a cabdriver chews a toothpick, choosing his words with care. No, it's not a happy time to visit Mexico. What set of interests is it, he wonders aloud, that brings people such as my wife and me to visit this side of the border. We're loyal to Mexico, I reply. We'd far prefer to leave our vacation dollars here than in Europe, or South America. You certainly do speak Spanish well, he remarks, his eyes narrowing. It seems a moment appropriate for my standard flip reply: so do you, I assure him. And with that, he releases a long whinny of a laugh, half swivels to face me, and apologizes for having thought that I was from the government. (Just which of the two governments did he think I represented? I'm never sure.)

He himself came to Juárez twenty years before, from Mexico City. He married a woman, it turns out, whose family lives here. Planning to open a little grocery store, year after year she and he saved what they could from his fares, while they put their four sons through various trade schools, while their four daughters married auto mechanics and plumbers and truckers, reliable fellows with steady work. And now all that planning seems about to vanish—if I will forgive the expression—in much the manner of a fart before a match flame. Two of his sons, and one of his sons-in-law, are out of work. All three men have gone north, to pick lettuce or apples or hops—no one's sure. All three wives, as well as eight of the grandchildren, now share with him and his wife the three-bedroom apartment they rent half a block behind the Plaza of Independence. *N'hombre,* this country is a perfect mess. The economy suffers from the same lack of leadership as the national soccer team that the country sends, every four years, to World Cup competition. The same lack of planning and discipline characterizes the thugs who control the ruling political party. Like sunlight blotting up puddles that glitter on street and sidewalk, inflation evaporates the savings a man has labored all his life to accumulate.

Wherever we aim our eyes, distractions and incongruities pluck at peripheral vision. The very sidewalks amount to one long study in cognitive dissonance. Barefoot Tarahumara Indian women, babies shawled, slung over one shoulder like carbines, stab their empty palms at the tourist. Octogenarians kneel on the steps of church or bank or department store, eyes downcast, muttering a half-audible *por dios, por el amor de dios*. Within six blocks our hands and pockets are full of flyers proposing strikes, or announcing protest marches. Loudspeakers rumble with news of organizational meetings. Posters attest to the bitterness that characterized the recent presidential election. One in particular catches our eye. A recently formed party ran, for president, the son of a former populist chief executive, now deceased. Demanding an end to the ruling party's antirevolutionary terrorism, the poster depicts a human hand that seizes by the tail and lifts a huge, snarling rat.

To counter inflation, the government issues bills of ever larger denominations, their colors ever more garish, their surfaces bearing portraits of heroes ever more obscure. As we sit in a dark bar over a beer, resting our senses a moment, a whole fistful of such bills, in denominations of fifty thousand, twenty thousand and ten, lies spread on the table before us, glowing like the fan of a coquette. Fingering a thousand-peso note, I try to explain to my wife how this scrap of paper releases, in a corner of my mind, a mild vertigo. Fifteen years ago, when worth eighty dollars, a thousand pesos paid a month's rent, or bought a couple of weeks' groceries. A fellow set out through downtown Guadalajara, armed with a single thousand-peso note, feeling himself ready for any eventuality. And today it's worth a little more than fifty cents U.S. It amounts to a tip appropriate for the old don in the faded, carefully ironed khakis who guards our car in the parking lot.

Wherever we go those lurid bills seem the principal topic of everyone's talk. They constitute the medium of exchange in a double sense, passing not only from pocket to pocket but, as well, in the form of conversation, from mind to mind. Idlers on park benches wonder aloud whether the outgoing president has managed to steal quite as much as his predecessor. To my wife the fellow operating a pottery stall offers no less a discount than 40 percent, if she'll only put away her credit card, and pay with those drab green dollars tucked into her billfold's corner. In vain we look for some official perspective, for any authority at all from which to pry a reliable set of facts.

The Juárez journalist squirms and stubs out one cigarette, then another. A friend of a friend, he's consented to chat about the current political turmoil as well as the growth, at the edge of town, of what they call along the border the *colonias*. Composed mainly of young men underemployed or out of work, fellows who've come north in hopes of crossing the border to work in Texas, or points even farther north, these squatter communities grow at the rate, he thinks, of a thousand a week. Their inhabitants live in cardboard or tar-paper lean-tos, without running water, with neither electricity nor sewer services even. Unspeakable crime and violence abound, he assures us. The impatience of the *colonos,* their resentment at their living conditions, produces the border's much-discussed political instability. In the election held six weeks ago, the ruling party's candidate did not win Chihuahua. The party has claimed victory; but no one at all believes the vote count. And what ever became of the ten thousand troops introduced a year ago to restore order after the mayoral election? Are the troops still here? Who knows, he shrugs, stubbing a cigarette.

He assures us that he exercises caution about what he says and writes. A chance remark in his weekly column might easily trigger a phone call, from any one of a number of anonymous observers, to any number of headquarters, down in the state capital, 150 miles south. News of his indiscretion might reach even as far as Mexico City. In any event, he remembers, he has at this very hour a pressing engagement. He must leave. He suggests that we talk further with his friend, an expert in border culture, an architect who has an office in the Municipal Palace. Looking through downtown Juárez for the palace, we ask a cabdriver, who in turn asks us whether we want the new one, or the old. We don't know, of course. Because it is nearer, we try the old one. Behind a steel desk, amid the rattle of manual typewriters, a secretary swears softly, wipes her face with a handkerchief, and announces that the man we seek now is officed across town, in the new Cultural Center. Negotiating a path through fumes from buses and trucks so old they run on the strength of prayers to the image of the Virgin of Guadalupe that graces each dashboard, we learn from a receptionist that the fellow we seek is in Mexico City, not to return till the end of the month. Yes, of course we can make an appointment to see him. If only we'll be good enough to return tomorrow morning, as his secretary has left for the day.

Across the street stands a federally sponsored crafts center. Tourists, mainly from the United States, browse over handicrafts that no longer would be produced, but for the government's subsidy of, and publicity for, the floor space on which they're sold. Next to pottery in the contrasting styles of Oaxaca and Jalisco stand *equipales,* those leather chairs of Aztec design, on one of which Montezuma sat to receive Cortés. We study the candle holders and cups of brass or tin, wall hangings woven of grass or palm leaf, mortar and pestle pairs made of volcanic stone, alabaster carvings, silver work. Into the woolen *zarapes,* as into the scarves, are woven motifs several centuries old. Especially vivid are two prehispanic forms of painting. The Huichol Indians coat a piece of plywood with beeswax, pressing onto it row after row of colored yarns that form designs, abstract or figurative, that sell for as much as several hundred dollars apiece. Other artists paint folk motifs on *amatl,* the ancient bark paper on which the Aztec and Mayan empires wrote their histories.

The border begins, after awhile, to wear out our eyes and ears, raw exhaustion reducing the sights and sounds to blur and noise. We study the scenes unwinding before us, now tranquil as a cathedral pew, now thrashing with sense impressions like a rush-hour intersection. Desperate to organize what assaults it, the mind begins to arrange everything in complementary pairs; our least observation calls out to some other scene, somewhere else, to throw it into relief. Consider the Tarahumara

61

men and boys, feathered and beribboned, dancing and drum-
ming up and down a Juárez sidewalk for spare change. The
Juárez authorities' toleration of them contrasts ironically with
certain antiloitering laws that govern the foot traffic of the poor
in downtown El Paso, where a friend of mine, for taking a nap
on a park bench, once spent a night in the county jail. Even
at the molecular level, the two sides of the river seem to seek
each other out. Rising off the Juárez streets, hydrocarbons in
the exhaust of cars twenty years old mingle hundreds of feet
in the air with sulfur fumes released from what the American
Smelting and Refining Company announced, twenty years ago,
was the world's tallest smokestack.

For the Juárez craft shop the mind locates a counterpart,
across the river, in various used-clothing stores that crowd
south El Paso. At a typical store a bell tinkles, the moment the
door opens, revealing no clerk anywhere in sight. From hangers
dangle row after row of jackets and dresses, abandoned, out-
dated, drab. Under signs marked *pantalón* and *camisa*, entire bins
of sleeves and legs spill on the floor in a tangled flight, shades of
khaki and white predominating, though here and there flow-
ered prints and garish checks do catch the eye. Down table after
table flows the underwear, a long, limp stream of white. Most
of these garments slip, sooner or later, across the border. So the
Juárez craft-shop glassblower, cheeks distended, sweating into
a secondhand polyester shirt, strains to shape a flower vase des-
tined to grace the window ledge of the El Paso accountant who
purchased the shirt, no doubt, when it first came in style.

And so a kind of equilibrium reigns. The handmade and the
manufactured, the crafted and the mass-produced, the border's
various products—like the lives that yield them—cling to a
balance perfectly precarious, tilting like a seismograph needle,
tipping and then recovering from each devaluation of the peso.

Seven hundred miles downstream, across the same muddy
river, another pair of towns face each other: Del Rio, Texas, and
Cd. Acuña, Coahuila. The former resembles a not-yet devel-
oped El Paso. Its wide residential streets, lined with big shade

trees, lend it the air of a prosperous farming community. Right up to the edge of parking lot and yard, irrigated fields unfurl. In front of the single Safeway, new pickups purr, keys dangling from their ignitions, the owners inside picking up a six-pack after work, secure in the belief they live in a town too small to support even a single auto thief. Acuña, though four times bigger than Del Rio, bears a population still only a tenth the size of that of Juárez, as well as a layout altogether more compact. To the sympathetic observer, both towns confide their secrets in a manner at once immediate and intimate, throwing into relief the far more massive, impersonal forces that form Juárez–El Paso.

Every bit as relaxed as our Juárez journalist was edgy, the curator of Acuña's municipal museum directs our attention to several hundred arrowheads he has mounted on display boards. On the wall hang photos of presidents, both Mexican and U.S., meeting nearby on various occasions of state. Now in his early sixties, retired to devote himself to the study of local history, the curator stiffens with pride while explaining that Acuña became, in 1908, the site of the very bloodletting that began the Revolution. Polished by years of repetition, the phrases slip from him like antique coins, throwing his shoulders back an inch, deepening his voice: *tierra y libertad, no reelección*. Even the name of the town he serves recalls a deed both intimate and violent, the death of Manuel Acuña, a poet who, in 1873, at age twenty-four, killed himself for love of a woman.

Acuña owes much of its current population to its *maquiladoras*, small, specialized factories which assemble foreign parts into products that afterward get shipped back to the United States. Our cursory count reveals no fewer than thirty-five such plants, each employing three shifts of workers. To list what the *maquiladoras* produce acknowledges their marginality, while suggesting as well that their presence here on the border owes wholly to all the cheap labor available. Their workers assemble disposable diapers, hospital caps and gowns, safety belts and car upholstery, toasters and blenders and fishing reels. They count coupons, and anodize aluminum. They turn out manikins, and the plastic rings for notebooks, shoes and slippers and automobile tires. For an eight-hour shift they receive the Mexican minimum daily wage of five dollars.

Many of the younger workers cruise the side streets, in cars and pickups the payments for which their wages must barely cover. Or they stroll the downtown, arm in arm, under a ragged blare of rock and roll from loudspeakers over the record stores. Most of the girls carry a child a year or two old, and the boys, a cassette player turned up loud enough to numb the teeth of the passerby. Whatever their chatter, it touches upon one topic over and over: somebody didn't get invited to a christening; and someone else hadn't even heard that she was pregnant. Moment by moment there rises, off these children of marginal industry, a tension openly, fiercely sexual. The dipping and gliding of their denim hips, their nimble feet and lively eyes: they signal from every angle how much and how often they want each other. Most no more than sixteen or eighteen years old, married already, with children to support, they might be some factory owner's fantasy, and a labor organizer's nightmare. In their energy and innocence and lust, they constitute an ever-renewable resource: a work force toiling by day for cheap wages, straining all night at each other in order to reproduce themselves.

Older workers, maybe more numerous, although less visible on the street, spend their days off at home, or out of town. The middle aged indeed often maintain one residence here in Acuña, as well as another farther south, in a state like Zacatecas or Guanajuato. In the latter, on a small farm, they plant corn or beans in the spring, returning to harvest in the fall. The rest of the year they work in a border-town *maquiladora*. Their seasonal migrations produce a corresponding difference in Acuña's population, a year-round count of some eighty thousand, as well as a floating population of perhaps another fifty thousand.

It is these latter workers whose numbers swell the ever-growing *colonias*. Typically, a man arrives by himself, and finds work in a *maquiladora*. Soon he and others like him, in an empty field at the edge of town, fling up shacks of corrugated tin or cardboard. Within months, they save enough to replace their flimsy walls with cinder block. And they hurry to do so. After all, when the field's owner, having invested in it for purposes of speculation, tries to get them evicted, the police will have more trouble demolishing cinder block than cardboard. However, if the authorities do succeed in evicting the squatters, the latter return immediately, and rebuild. The owner can rarely afford to pay the police for round-the-clock protection. So a worker's persistence sooner or later wins him a residence.

Having gained a foothold, however extralegal, on land owned by someone else, the workers immediately write home with the news that lots are available. Within weeks they're joined by their wives and children, as well as by compadres and cousins and friends, all of whom soon find work and fling up, in turn, their own structures. Within a matter of months, a *colonia* that began with a dozen or so workers has grown to a thousand. Soon it comes time for the municipal elections. Officials of the competing parties outdo each other in promising running water, sewer lines, electricity. The *colonos,* of course, vote as a block for whoever makes the best offer.

One night in a restaurant we strike up a conversation with the manager. A native of Mexico City, he himself has come to Acuña only a year and a half before. There simply came a time, he shrugs, when he had to remove his wife and kids from the violence and congestion that by now characterize life in the capital. His brother and sister-in-law already lived here, so he and his family decided to take the chance. His name is José. He is thirty-nine. By being both younger and newer to the border, he presents an instructive contrast to the Juárez cabby with whom we chatted.

He sips cup after cup of black coffee, and toys with his wedding band, recalling how his first job here amounted to tending bar in a whorehouse. Within months he was lucky enough to secure his present position, the salary from which, however, barely covers tuition for the son he has in Monterrey studying to be an engineer. The more that José and I compare our impressions of border life, the more of them we find we have in common. For him, too, the contrasts are garish, and perfectly unpredictable. Like us, he often finds himself trapped between laughter and tears, rebounding from admiration to revulsion, ambushed by embarrassment, or by pride. The following afternoon, it turns out, he has an errand to run. He's driving over to one of the very newest and rawest of the *colonias*. He wonders if we might not like to go along.

The dirt road the next day leaves our car trailing a hundred-foot plume of dust. Wherever we look, naked children and skinny dogs slink in and out of the shadows. Before each shack sits the fifty-gallon drum the city fills twice a week with water. Here vans from the *maquiladoras* pick up and deposit workers. There laundry droops from clothes lines, and smoke climbs from charcoal cooking fires. As night brings no relief from the suffocating humidity, a bed or two sags in each front yard. Behind the settlement stretch acres of brush to be cleared overnight, by men with machetes, newly arrived, ready to throw together other dwellings, ready to assemble more foreign parts. Such *colonias*, José assures us, represent the future of a nation unable to make work for its young and its campesinos. Indeed, the government strictly regulates all wages hereabouts. Otherwise the entire republic's population would rush to the border, tipping the economy even further off balance.

And yet, *maquiladoras* represent but one way the locals adapt to the rigors of making a living. An adaptation equally common amounts to the practice of *coyotaje*. If the former involves importing menial jobs, the latter exports illegals into such jobs north of the river. A trade every bit as honorable as that plied by the carpenter or the bricklayer, and far less subject to economic fluctuations, *coyotaje* tends to pass from father to son, generation to generation. Most of the families who practice it, José confides, live in a neighborhood named El Porvenir, a term which means, appropriately enough, "the future."

El Porvenir amounts to a section of town, some eight-by-ten

blocks in size, composed of dusty, unpaved streets that wind and climb and fall among single-story cinder-block houses perhaps six rooms in size. Each has a narrow front yard and patio, the former of packed dirt, the latter frequently concrete. A shade tree often guards the front door, and sometimes a waist-high cinder-block fence as well. The *maquiladora* vans halt at the neighborhood's edge, depositing their riders, only to make a respectful turn and leave. The police pay but the most hurried visits, on urgent matters, and only during daylight. Nothing, José assures us, could ever persuade a cop to remain after dark in El Porvenir. Five or so years old, most often with plates from California or Texas, large Chevys and Fords and Dodges sag like beasts of burden in driveways, or at curbside. And beasts of burden they are. Each gets periodically fitted, in place of trunk and back seat, with special compartments in which six or eight aliens ride north for several hundred miles. Heavy-duty shock absorbers prevent the car from riding so low as to give away the presence of its cargo.

The prospective alien takes up residence, first, in a safe house on the Mexican side, protected from the federal police charged with preventing illegals from crossing the border. In a matter of days, when a group of ten to fifteen has assembled, they get led after dark across the river, at any of various shallow places, to a safe house on the U.S. side. Divided there into groups of five or six, according to destination, they ride north in sedans equipped to accommodate them, dodging the *migra*, or U.S. Immigration and Naturalization Service, by maneuvers both plentiful and ingenious. A common ploy involves the use of scout cars. Different vehicles get sent down each of three or four highways. Since their limited manpower lets the *migra* observe at most two of the roads, the driver who travels an unwatched highway telephones a message in code, and a vehicle bearing its human cargo travels that route non-stop to the destination. Another method involves sending past the *migra* a driver who feigns drunkenness. While the officials have him pulled over, a sedan bearing illegals slips by.

The day before we're due to leave for home, we take a stroll through downtown Acuña. Lined with benches and shade trees, five sidewalks wander through the central plaza and up to the bandstand. On each a head-high pedestal bears the bust of a national hero. On the benches we find sitting the very young and the very old. Here and there among them we find men of working age, newly arrived at the bus station, three blocks away. Now they wait to meet some *coyote,* in order to cross the river to Dallas, or Houston, or San Antonio. They carry no more than a knapsack or a suitcase, as well as twenty thousand pesos or so with which they'll eat while on the road. The looks that cross their faces range from wariness to weariness.

We amble over to a municipal park, and stand at river's edge, looking toward Del Rio. I wonder how many journeys begin with a step into the muddy ripples slipping past my feet, as well as how many travelers aim north from here, or northwest really, hoping to pick the apples that sweeten up and down the basalt slopes, two thousand miles away, within sight of our front yard.

The principle of the binary has bound together, sometimes with a twisted irony, all that my wife and I have noticed. The contrasting, the complementary—whatever we've observed has occurred in the kind of pairs that my memory of this area prepared us to apprehend. Each of our observations has felt half-transitional, a dip of attention from one act of noticing to another, our each perception throwing some other into a momentary clarity. It even occurs to me that maybe the border itself amounts to nothing more than a tangle of shifting boundaries. By now I'm eyeing sunlit water crossed by people for whom this landscape forms, with that other, two thousand miles north, an apparently endless succession of borders. I suspect the United States amounts to no more than a lengthening ripple effect, receding in all directions from the step of whoever enters it.

I even understand that I myself, at this moment, represent a certain kind of transition. I amount to little more than a shortcut time has taken: from the kid who eyed this very river twenty-five years ago, to the man already planning to describe this moment, months from now, behind a study window from which he can see almost to Canada. And yet however relative the terms in which the border demands description, I know it does represent, as well, a kind of absolute. I think of those Laredans of a century and a half ago. To them it mattered so much on which side of this water the bodies of those they loved decomposed that they carried out the one spiteful, grandiose gesture for which, to this very day, we remember them. Like them I respond to absolute difference as much as I do to degrees of transition. Certain of my likes and dislikes survive any relativity wrung from the past and the future. I pervade, in fact, whatever I observe.

For example the border, for these three weeks, has seemed by far more Mexican than Anglo. Its active ingredients, anyway, have seemed again and again to derive from south of the river; the U.S. side has served as little more than a kind of background, providing the raw material of contrast. And yet the apparent predominance of Mexico owes, in fact, to the company of my wife: I've been looking, in large measure, through her eyes. Had I come here not from the home that she and I share, but rather from Guadalajara—in the company of my godson, say, who's never even seen the United States—why, the border viewed under those conditions would have looked very different indeed. I no doubt would've noticed the money-changing houses, and the greater proportion of new automobiles, both signs to the Mexican traveler headed north that he or she approaches the edge of the world's greatest accumulation of wealth. I probably would've prowled the countryside north of the river, interviewing people in English, observing an altogether different set of contrasts. The familiar and the exotic would interplay of course, regardless of which direction I were headed, no matter with whom I observed the border, no matter which language we spoke. But no matter how many different figure-ground reversals of culture flickered through my mind, I do believe I'd recall those stubborn citizens of Laredo. Our crossing of any border owes, after all, as much to what we abandon as it does to what we anticipate.

TWO LOVE SCENES
IN HOMER

The *Iliad*, we hear in the opening lines, rings with one man's anger. The slight of a moment—Agamemnon seizing the girl Achilleus was awarded—brings on the Akhaians week after week of slow-motion death. The wise and foolish alike, aglitter in armor and patronymics, the foolhardy and the sorrowful, a man torn through the spleen by a spear, another whose severed head drops, talking yet, to the dust underfoot—their chiseled differences leave more poignant the fact of the same darkness falling over each.

There I go again. I've just spent nine months talking to twenty-year-olds about the *Iliad*, about a series of deaths they barely can imagine, however hard they try. And try they do. So by now, late August, my wife and I have slipped off some three thousand miles, to a cove on the Pacific coast of Mexico, to rest, and wouldn't you know it? Those Bronze Age speeches won't let go of my mind. I'll catch myself at the breakfast table comparing my own most recent dream to that of Agamemnon, the one from which he took that disastrous advice to continue stubbornly plying his trade, there by the edge of the sea. Or I'll glance at a bowl of pineapple slices, and remember that the very first bowl got molded on one of Helen's breasts. So three thousand miles from my battered copy of it, the poem maintains an elusive control of me, one I can neither dismiss nor define. I think how death seems one dark mist, to each of the heroes, however different their lives. And I think how we go swimming every morning about eleven. I half dread and half thrill at that first plunge under, the moment I make a green cliff or my wife's face, whatever I see last, turn into the darkness. It even occurs to me that I'm practicing—without especially wanting to—a kind of compulsive literary criticism. Much as some ancient mariner might wander around, seeing in any event an occasion to narrate what happened to him, I seem intent on making of this beach, and everything on it, one elaborate marginal comment on that other, invisible beach.

Over all differences in the *Iliad* reigns the painful, brooding figure of Achilleus. He is the greatest hero. And his own stature, after Agamemnon's moment of pettiness, becomes his insoluble problem. He must exact from Agamemnon something equivalent in value to the diminishment of his honor. Yet for him to name a price would allow us—the men and women he knows will be watching, from other times and lands—would force us, indeed, to wonder why he didn't ask for even more. He has practically willed himself into being. He has given himself the task of becoming the greatest hero we can imagine. Akhaians and Trojans alike, Hektor himself in fact, all depend on his living up to his own demands on himself. To die remains inevitable, and bitter. But to die alongside, or even at the hands of, the great Achilleus—this propels a man quite beyond his own death. So our hero must set his price cunningly.

It is in Book IX that we first see him struggle to do so. To coax him back to the fighting, Agamemnon has made an offer: a kingdom, a daughter's hand in marriage, wealth—I don't remember what. He offers as well to return the girl, untouched, it turns out. (Didn't Agamemnon know, even at the moment of their quarrel, that he would end up returning her?) The offer is brought to Achilleus's tent by a delegation cleverly put together: Odysseus, the eloquent tactician; Phoinix, an aged countryman much like a father to Achilleus; and that Aias who is, but for Achilleus himself, the finest fighting man of all Akhaia. Odysseus speaks first. He details Agamemnon's offer, item by item. He adds that Achilleus has an obligation to save those who came here with him. And in a final, perhaps unintended thrust, he mentions that Hektor would not right now, in hot blood, be as difficult to kill as before. The reply is rigid with contempt. Achilleus announces he hates, in Richmond Lattimore's phrase, the man who hides one thing in his heart and speaks another. He hates him like the gates of death. Not only will he not reenter the fighting: the Akhaians will see, at dawn tomorrow, his ships under sail for home, glittering on the Hellespont. Then Phoinix rises to speak. His argument comes spun from a past both cultural and personal. He offers the analogy of Meleagros, who, belittled by a ruler much his inferior, accepted for the common good a peace offering, and fought to save his comrades. Phoinix points out that his own life is in danger. Might Achilleus not consider the safety of the man who reared him? And now the reply feels softer. A bed for the night, Achilleus offers the old man, and passage home the next day. The bitterness has fallen out of his voice; but he'll not take up arms again. Finally, Aias speaks. The briefest of the three, his speech runs but a few lines. He accuses Achilleus of having slipped quite beyond the edge of human custom. Tradition dictates, he says, that a man accept the blood price from even his own brother's murderer: that any desire for vengeance must give way to the ongoing needs of society. Achilleus, he suggests, bears a bit too much of the cold gray sea in him—that very medium through which his immortal mother, Thetis, works her way. And suddenly, Achilleus does what he can to relent. He will enter the fighting again, but only when it comes near enough, and only to defend his own ships. So the visitors depart; their interview is over. Yet

we notice it wasn't that argument of Odysseus, about the risk
of losing glory, that changed the hero's mind; nor was it that of
Phoinix, that he risked uncivilized behavior. No, it is the blunt
lines of Aias, gnarled with assumptions only the two of them
can hear, that keep Achilleus on the beach.

A proud man has changed his mind a little: yet at the risk of
devaluating his personal honor, which, nearly alone, has made
it worth the others' lives to be here. Akhaian and Trojan alike
stand to lose, if he cheapens himself. Before we have so much
as seen him lift a sword, we intuit why he's become the great-
est hero. He understands honor. Indeed perhaps only Aias is
his equal, in understanding its demands. When Aias implied
Achilleus had grown as detached as an immortal, he hinted at a
truth so dark we suspect only the two of them can fully under-
stand: the gods themselves, who cannot die, can entertain but
the dimmest notion of honor. They have nothing to risk. But
Achilleus too, if he leaves, has nothing to risk. So he stays. His
love of being a man, rather than a god—that is what overcomes
his scorn for Odysseus, his hatred of Agamemnon. Finally, we
understand, we have witnessed a kind of love scene.

The courtliness of the scene feels Mexican, somehow. The glib
and self-serving Odysseus, the poignant Phoinix, the laconic yet
finely intuitive Aias—the passion of each gets thrown into relief
against Achilleus's tact, and his hospitality. Replying to Odys-
seus, even, he remains utterly courtly. His example reminds me
that in a culture where manners are valued, a kind of transpar-
ent equality follows men about: the wronged and the wrong-
doer, the wealthy man and the poor. A peasant may have better
manners than a president.

I think of don Venancio, the gardener where I lived years
ago in Guadalajara. Well over seventy-five, he arrived every
two weeks, lawnmower and sickle roped to an old bicycle. He
trimmed the grass and spaded the flowerbeds. The lime and
guayaba and orange trees were his alone to prune, and to train.
But often he liked to talk: endless tales of his days in the Revo-
lution, as a Carrancista. Any topic whatever could lead, in one

or two deft moves, to his announcing with a sigh that it was a day very much like this, young man, when we retook Guadalajara. He could recall the machine-gun bullets whining through knee-high grass. He remembered a horse an officer lent him. But finally one day over a Coke, he approached a more personal past. His oldest son, some ten or fifteen years ago, had been contract murdered by a local *político*. Over a woman, he thought. Off to the university he had sent this boy, who was even going to be a lawyer, until that fellow had him killed. I'm terribly sorry, I said. *Pos' no,* amigo, he nodded and emptied the bottle. He picked up a spade. All is not lost, it turns out. I have learned where that man lives. I know that he goes to work every day down a certain deserted street.

For all his manners, as we have seen, Achilleus can bear no double talk. And yet the debate in Book IX, and maybe the nature of dialogue itself, demand that kind of straightforwardness, both in words and appearance, of which Odysseus is rarely capable—preferring, as he does, a life of lies and disguises. Are we right to sense between our heroes the conflict of the literal with the figurative? Perhaps. In any event, the character of Odysseus gets revealed in another dialogue, one he conducts with Athene, in Book XIII, of the *Odyssey.* We can see him learning to live among men and women again, after nearly twenty years away. Phaikian sailors have left him asleep beside the splendid gifts his stories have won him. On the beach of his home, Ithaka, he wakes alone, complaining bitterly that the Phaikians have robbed him. He spies the gifts, then, but still doesn't recognize where he is. Suddenly, he notices a tall young man ambling down the beach. And Odysseus smiles. We know it is Athene, because Homer has told us so. But could Odysseus know? He proceeds to tell the young man a lie so farfetched that, in laughing, the youngster reveals himself as Athene: only someone who knew this was Odysseus could have thought the story amusing. (But, if Odysseus knew, why not merely address her as who she was? Because she is deeply proud of her skill at disguises!) You really didn't recognize me, she chides him, admiring the lie that made her laugh. Of course not, he replies. I didn't even recognize you, back there in Phaikia, disguised as a little girl. But wait, we remember—she never had revealed herself to him there; twice now, he's seen through her efforts. We can imagine her pique. Her response is to invent for him a disguise that amounts to no disguise at all. She strips away the rugged good looks that had won the heart of Nausikaa; she leaves him looking worn, ill-used by the world, a ragged and weary tramp. In short, she makes him seem the very beggar that his enemies would know he has become, by now, if he's still alive. But why, we wonder, did he try to match wits with her? Does it disgrace him that he lost? Or that our lady of strategies has favored him with a disguise that will earn him jeers and blows? Not really. His is the love of being different men, who is no man at all. He is rather the quick separations between a man and himself.

To me Odysseus recalls another changeable man. Skip was fifty-five when I knew him first, a black man from Texas, the grandson of slaves. He'd maybe run a string of women in Houston in the thirties. Maybe he'd even done time. But now—always a ferocious reader and talker—he'd fallen into the employ of a sociology department, in a small Northwest college. He had no degrees, only that eerie, limitless energy of the largely self-educated. Nothing came too tediously for him: he prowled their library like a tomcat in a salmon cannery. His classes were exercises in social imagination: he required the students to interview pimps and policemen, dealers and parish priests. He died only a month ago, abruptly, of a stroke. For fifteen years we had known each other.

The college administrators who hired him could never have understood the metaphoric man they employed. He spoke his mind anywhere, and often. His politics alone, a rarified blend of Marxism and sarcasm, would have done it. But he drank, as well, and gloriously, without excuse or apology. We were together a lot. So I don't remember when exactly it started, his very own way of ambushing the deans with their own expectations: he merely began wearing overalls. Of course many youngsters flitted through the sixties in overalls and bare feet. But here came a sixty-year-old colleague, all beard and overalls, a copy of Herodotus under one arm. And worst of all, the colleague walked around perfectly toothless. (Did he own false teeth, even? I never asked.) So he came to resemble a field hand, yet every now and then his speech broke into a dazzling range of tones. He dearly loved that riff from abstract analyst to country boy and back.

Of the dean who slighted him most, remarkably little calls out to be noted. A short, thick-neck Ph.D., all ex-Marine officer, his ego and eyeglasses and mustache lent him a permanent San Juan Hill swagger. He would of course have considered himself merely decisive. Forever, he condescended to Skip, who in turn hated every inch of him. Finally a dismissal occurred; then a legal battle which, a year ago, Skip won. And so he resumed his classes. We'd meet half by accident in a parking lot or bar, and talk old times, and laugh at fools, and laugh like fools.

It is early evening. My wife has gone into town. I'm standing alone on our balcony, rum and Coke in hand. A few days more, it occurs to me, and I'll crouch at a desk at work, half a continent away. Already I catch myself looking out to sea in the direction, or I hope it was, in which men flickered, departing for that other world where men can be no more than stories— where I myself will be, in these pages, no more than the story I'm telling.

Indeed it is in this other world, we learn from one of Odysseus's stories, where he and Achilleus meet, for one last time. Achilleus is some years dead now; Odysseus has come only to ask the advice of a dead prophet. The story is one Odysseus tells to the Phaikians: he very much needs to impress them, and having Achilleus respect him here, in his story, would further things, surely.

But Achilleus shows him no great respect. He corrects Odysseus's foolish sense of how it must feel to be dead. He asks for news of his son, on earth. And hearing the son has won men's respect, he strides off through those plains of asphodel, leaving Odysseus, forever, in mid-remark. How very like him that Achilleus, even trapped in the mouth of a consummate liar, will act like no one but himself. And how very like Odysseus to tell us that. For they are not opposites, entirely. They represent the love of being a man, as against the love of being a fine story.

AMERICAN
MIRACLES

*Wherefore in memory of them we ought to honor any relic
of theirs in a fitting manner. . . . Hence God himself
honors such relics by working miracles in their presence.*
—St. Thomas Aquinas, *Summa Theologica*

Three days before his sixty-ninth birthday, at home in Camden, New Jersey, Walt Whitman was refusing dinner invitations. Three this week in fact. Tonight Horace Traubel had come by with news from the printer about *November Boughs*. Now the talk drifted toward the refusal of a mutual friend to pay his taxes. He's like Thoreau, Walt remarked, why should they pay taxes to a government they don't believe in? Yes why should they? he warmed to the topic. And it's also so—why shouldn't they? Didn't you tell me once Thoreau refused to pay and went to jail up there in Massachusetts? It seems like kicking against night and day—the course of nature—the rainfall.

By now, Horace was scribbling unobtrusively on a bit of paper pulled from his coat pocket. Probably he thought to make a book of these conversations. Well why not? Thoreau, like Horace, had been a decent fellow, and though his expectations ran a bit high, he remained direct, and plain. Like the time he'd come to the Whitman house in Brooklyn for a little conversation, and finding Walt not at home, had brushed by the startled Mrs. Whitman on into her kitchen to pull from the oven two cakes that only now had begun to burn, while he'd stood chatting at the door. But that moment lay forty years and a hundred miles away. Tonight, as the spring breeze up and down Mickle Street fetched a whiff of the fertilizer plant across the river, Walt thought how he'd dwelt in this house for only four years, though now he rarely left it. Horace and one of the young men with him began to chat about a certain pee-a-nist. As if from another room, the poet heard himself laugh, Do you mean a pianner player? Well now, in general, the instrument seems quite unequal to the big things. Then feeling rather than seeing their frown, he caught himself. I know, I know the obvious retort is that I have never really heard it played. That may be true. I wouldn't go to the stake for my opinion on this subject.

It is 1985. The voting booth has become our instrument least equal to the big things. With tiny, insurrectionary twitches of rage we leave it; we let out our feelings by intoning picket-sign rhymes at one another. But not long ago, I thought to avoid all the frustration. The morning of our most recent exercise in self-deception, I got up before dawn, and set out jogging through empty streets and alleys. Not even the trig Doberman who intercepts and escorts the foreign odor of me from his territory, growling lightly with the bother, not even he was awake. High overhead, two crows grated like matches being struck. What was the hurry? I had hours to run myself into the pleasant blur of attitude I needed to open the curtain to that booth. Gray November America spilled, oozed, and flapped into place along a roadbed from which the discouraged Chicago, Milwaukee and something had long since pried both ties and rails and vanished. A big Holstein groaned and shook herself. I was sweating free of my own stiff body, little by little. Now I could go indoors to fill their ballot with X's, dripping on it, and even fold it for them.

I remembered, as I ran, Walt's vow to wear his hat indoors or out as he pleased. It recalled that other lovely Quaker, William Penn, who had failed in the presence of Charles II to remove his hat, and so prompted the king himself to uncover. But Friend Charles, why dost thou not keep on thy hat? purred Friend William. His subtle monarch, who only recently had brought the prophylactic from the French court to the English, replied it was custom here for only one man at a time to retain his hat. Even the bandanna around my brow dripped in delight. I could feel the two of them, off in what they knew already was history, half mincing at each other. Friend William's mathematical plainness had laid the streets of Philadelphia so firmly in a gridiron pattern that, even today, the weedy sidewalks at my feet crossed at right angles. Horace Traubel would have looked right across the Delaware River at Philadelphia. But Penn's green haven unto oddballs, from where Horace sat, was only the fertilizer odor at a poet's window.

What is a bit of headgear anyway? Had I been twenty miles east, in the Columbia River Gorge, I likely would've been puzzling over my favorite petroglyphs. Four or five governors ago, the state lifted them up behind a little steel fence, out of what had been their original perch, a couple hundred feet over that black water, out where men had clung in the wind to daub a bit of colored animal fat onto the black basalt. The figures seem mainly horned animals, prey hoped for, or remembered gratefully, the painter himself maybe not sure which. But among all that curved animal alertness, there do stand a few stick men, each with long rays proceeding from his head. And it does make a fellow wonder. How tightly we maintain one ancient visual habit—that of believing the godlike among us bear some irregularity about the head, a crown or halo, a tonsure or feathered bonnet. All nodding in and out of the same poses.

Not to frighten even more his tiny son, who one day was going to inherit all of Troy, Hektor laughed and lay his tall horsehair helmet on a parapet. On the rubble of which the Greeks would later take care to dash out the boy's brains. A whole generation of my very own countrymen lurched awake watching a young president's haircut fly apart.

✿

In approving the veneration of relics, the Council of Trent laid forever under glass a few bones and scraps of cloth. But what greater devotion lies on display in a small mining town a thousand miles south of Albuquerque, in the Sierra Madre. Exotic minerals lace the ground, down there. A single silver mine at the edge of town yielded, for fifty years, two centuries ago, 80 percent of all the world's silver. In a cemetery at another end of town, rainwater steeped in the rocky soil mummifies about every hundredth body. Aged and newborn alike, the poor whose plot rent has gone too long unpaid get pried out of dirt that has left them replicas of themselves. Nearly a hundred recline or stand propped up in cases in a display room: so many white beards, a woman buried with belly flapping open from a cesarean. Many of the parchment faces bear a look of utter terror. A local legend suggests they fell prey to a landslide. But we know better. We recognize their expression. Caught, like us, in the act of learning another use the living find for the dead, they cringe. Out front the sign reads Panteón Municipal.

✿

A rhetoric of relics, maybe we need only that, to objectify ourselves. Consider how people drive great distances to sit beneath the retired jerseys of heroes and cheer. The heirloom is a kind of talking object. My grandfather knew a man who, on a long journey by Pullman, half-asleep one morning, borrowed a hairbrush from another fellow's shaving kit. Because a couple of razor blades had gotten tangled in it, he brushed his scalp to pieces. Just like that, without explanation, the story stayed in our family as a kind of heirloom.

But sometimes we catch events in the process of becoming family stories. I was yawning in a coffee shop one Sunday morning. At the next table slumped a young man eyeing a geography textbook. A trail of crumbs from the doughnut on the napkin before him sprouted down the page he read. Then the door opened, and a dapper, white-haired little wino sat beside him. Learning that the youngster planned to become a music teacher, our visitor plucked the pleat of his shiny flannel trousers and announced, When I was your age, there was nothing I wanted to be, 'cause there was already enough of everything there was.

Horace Traubel wrote a very fine book. Four volumes, direct as the breeze from Philadelphia that night. He could've called it Walt Lets Down His Hair, the old man so glows with common sense. Whitman's faintly pompous tone, from time to time, becomes endearing when we recall all that Horace must have expected, demanded even, in the way of guru-ship from a man who was really only a tired writer now. A writer left hostage to youngsters who admired a character he had created. Everyone envied Walt's health. But soon enough, they could read the autopsy: the left lung collapsed, with only an eighth of the right at all capable of breath. An abscess had so eaten through the fifth rib on the left side that it grated when moved. A huge stone filled the gallbladder, and tubercles the kidneys, intestines, and liver. For at least three months he lived like that, without a syllable of complaint. He died one rainy afternoon with his right hand in that of Horace Traubel. Their volumes of collaboration let us belong to that raw breeze at the window, the mounds of manuscript on the floor, the air brimming with subtle pauses, subtler yet each change of topic. Let us remember Horace and Walt as piano player and player piano, alternately, instrument, performer.

WHERE PIGS
CAN SEE THE WIND

The etymological meaning of superstitio *is perhaps*
"standing over a thing in amazement or awe."
—*Oxford English Dictionary*

I go for years without thinking about it. And then, for no apparent reason, I suddenly recall a belief common among Missouri hill folk when I was growing up. They used to say that a sound like that of glass breaking, or cloth tearing, presages a death in the family. I certainly don't believe it the way they did. But the moment their belief trails through my mind, I do feel a certain satisfaction. I also feel it when I recall their notion that hiding, under the bed, either a knife or a skillet makes the couple sleeping there conceive, respectively, either a boy or a girl. There's something plain satisfying about the belief that the touch of a dead man's hand will clear up a girl's complexion.

Or that eating bread crusts will leave her hair curly. These are very old notions, of course. Maybe their age explains the mix of skepticism and sympathy they elicit from people like me.

Maybe we savor superstitions the way we would an aged wine, or the dish yielded by a hundred-year-old recipe, to divert the palate with a bit of time travel. Many of us, anyhow, do delight in sampling habits of mind from another age; indeed, we find that our memories retain folk beliefs like cockleburs. I confess to owning five or six volumes of such material. Another eight or ten, checked out of the library, often sprawl on my desk or lurk under my chair, after I've spent the day grading papers, or preparing a lecture on Homer. I'm certainly not a trained folklorist. So it fascinates me, this delight I take in observing with "amazement or awe" the superstitions of others. I'll bet it amounts to a habit of mind every bit as exotic as those I observe.

I like to wonder how it was that such beliefs originated. Consider that one about binding a madstone, found in the entrails of a deer, to the bite of a rabid dog to suck out the poison. Or consider the suspicion that the family cat, given half a chance, will suck the breath from a baby. Surely no single person invented these notions. In fact, they attract me precisely because they represent a shared, inherited wisdom, anonymous as ballads. Each has a history, no doubt, but a history we can reconstruct only by research resembling that which etymologists train on a word. So various scholars have traced the throwing of spilled salt over the left shoulder to a belief, common among the ancients, that salt, because of its power to preserve against decay, represented the forces of life. We thwart the destruction of life, symbolized when we spill salt, by throwing a pinch into the face of the powers of evil hovering at our "sinister" side. An equally ancient notion that the reflection amounts to another self, or soul, yields our belief that a broken mirror brings bad luck to the one who breaks it.

It's tempting to view folk notions as something like truncated rituals, the vestigial organs of belief. They survive in the public performance of a custom, in our launching a ship, for example, by breaking a bottle of wine across its bow; but they survive as well in our knocking on wood, in our little compulsive tics the performance of which is not just individual, but indeed half-surreptitious. Maybe, in observing a custom, we only acknowledge the expectations of others. After all, the rice we throw at a wedding, the flowers we leave at a funeral, the horseshoe or antlers nailed over our doorway, our handshake, the tip of our hat—what are they but ruins of once-elaborate psychic systems? Like those toppled faceted stones that vivify the Mexican landscape, they keep the mind aimed at its own past. Still, in yielding to a superstition, we do half-acknowledge the existence of something like supernatural factors. If I fail to flip a pinch of spilled salt over my shoulder, I may feel no more than vaguely uncomfortable. But at other times my mind will slip for an instant, and leave me suspecting that we ourselves amount to no more than so many host organisms, a kind of fleshy medium by means of which our beliefs perpetuate and permutate themselves.

The westernmost counties of Illinois, where I grew up, have furnished material for several collections of folk beliefs. I couldn't tell you how many times I've looked at these volumes. It feels like revisiting my childhood, when I read again the pages on which common objects become animate, where mute things turn articulate. The moment a sentence reminds me, I remember all over again how a singing chimney warns of a change in the weather, or that clothes lines turn taut, and teakettles sweat, to foretell rain. Cornhusks and onion skins, grown thicker than usual, presage a harsh winter; and so do the activities of squirrels, if they build their nests larger and deeper. Even shoes squeak to warn that a storm approaches.

Nameless informants, people whose memories yielded these pages, recall the beliefs that meandered through their lives. Fellows remember lubricating their hunting rifles with rabbit grease, or turning their pockets inside out to catch catfish. A barber swears a sick man, shaved in bed, will suffer a setback; and a circus roustabout, that whoever drives the first stake will find money. A miner allows as how, if the light on your cap goes out when you enter the mine, you'll never come out alive. The owner of a rooming house, in order to rent them, scrubs the floors of her vacant rooms with saltwater.

Sometimes the same cause will yield utterly different effects. Mother's milk squirted into a baby's eyes cures pinkeye; or it brings on blindness. More often, the same phenomenon springs from utterly different portents: both large raindrops and small cucumbers signal imminent death; singing in the bathroom brings rain, but so does dragging your swing to a stop with both feet. Either transplanting a cedar tree, or stepping over a dead snake, will bring on the death of a family member. Burning a bit of palm branch blessed on Palm Sunday protects against being hit by lightning. But so does wearing your suspenders crossed.

Paging through all this material produces a sensation nearly tactile, a feel of different textures rippling beneath the mind. Pretty soon, I don't care whether anyone ever believed in the notions I'm reading. What is it, after all, to "believe" that sleeping on ironed sheets will make us peevish? "Interpret a dream of a large grain field as a happy marriage," a page tells me; and only a moment later I learn that "sorrow follows a dream of eating cabbage." Maybe I read for the kinetic excitement of image yielding to image. It massages otherwise unreachable corners of your spirit, maybe, when you learn that a butterfly in the house foretells a woman visitor, and a flea on your hand, a letter. Killing a cricket makes your teeth rot; and placing three lice from your head in a coffin obliges the corpse to carry all your other lice away. Hairs from a horse's tail, left in rainwater, grow into snakes. A violin will maintain its tone if you keep inside it the rattles you've cut off a rattlesnake. A crow, if you split its tongue, can learn to talk. Many a sporting woman, for luck, tucks a spider into her right stocking. The person who manages to throw a feather over a house will find a lot of money on the other side. After licking a dead man's blood, any dog will go mad. Cats draw lightning. Pigs can see the wind.

The pages I read contain some ten or twenty thousand entries, grouped by topic and variation. The collectors make no effort to organize their material into patterns resembling those of daily experience. Yet every once in a while, from between and behind such entries, I do catch glimpses of an entirety, a whole world that, although not identical to our own, certainly does proceed in a self-consistent fashion. Often I try to fit these observations together, to make a composite world of all the folk notions I read. And when I do I see a landscape built of shifting boundaries, one in which any object amounts to no more than a vague zone of transition between itself and what it seems in the process of becoming: in order to begin wriggling and hissing, horsehairs lack only immersion in rainwater; only its joined tongue prevents the crow from learning to speak to us. What's more, any given element attracts some other, albeit one with properties different from its own. So an affinity for the most spectacular, least tamable element of our weather, the lightning bolt, distinguishes that furtive domestic animal, the cat. The ability to see the wind belongs to no sylphlike, otherworldly creature; rather, it characterizes something that lives by grunting and rooting through our refuse.

Human flesh seems to represent a transition between mind and matter, the angle of attraction between belief and body, as if the leverage the one exerts on the other used our skin as a fulcrum. So body type yields information pertaining to personality. Those with broad shoulders are carefree, and those with large mouths and thin lips can foretell the future. Low-voiced persons, or those with sunken eyes, are given to deceit. Hair on the body signifies strength, and a mole on the buttocks portends death by hanging. Almost at will, we can change the body: their breasts will enlarge if girls eat chicken gizzards; drinking goat's milk will give them personality. We even can learn to whistle by eating burnt bread. And like our body types, our apparently least significant acts betray our deepest motives.

Whatever thought we happen to entertain while sneezing will come true. The person who talks to himself or herself is talking to the devil.

In the world that I glimpse when I piece together different folk beliefs, time itself admits of no fixed boundaries. The future lies implicit in the present. So certain people—those born in November, the prophet's month—have the gift of foretelling, as do those born with a "veil," or a caul. But portents surround the rest of us as well, whether they take the form of animal behavior, or that of the images in our dreams. Even the dead differ from the living more in degree than they do in kind. So a man who has drowned floats facedown, and a woman, faceup: we mimic in death the positions appropriate, in lovemaking, to our genders. (Except that, out of shame, the pregnant but unwed girl who drowns will float facing downward.) Often enough, at the very moment we die, we appear to loved ones miles away, as if space itself were only some illusion that the living entertained.

In the westernmost counties of Illinois, witches are men and women who manipulate the vagueness of all of life's boundaries. With no more than a phrase, they travel huge distances. Behexing us, they shift their shapes to that of a pig or a deer, a rabbit or a snake, even a fly. Their conjures leave our children braying or bleating or howling. Every time they're angry, they need to cast a spell; by removing it, we make them suffer, and they visit us to complain. Our horses balk at the roads witches have traveled recently. Witches inhabit our churns, till the butter won't come; they slip feather wreaths into our pillows, to weaken us. Holding in their mouths the neckbone of a black cat they've boiled alive, witches can turn themselves invisible.

These beliefs derive from a certain landscape—from the Mississippi River, its bluffs, and the sky—and in particular from Quincy, the seat of the county of Adams. Today Quincy remains very much what it was during my childhood, a dying river town lined with padlocked factory gates and hundred-year-old brick walls. Its maple-tree avenues offer, at nearly every corner, some beer joint with a name like the Dew Drop Inn. Every summer, miles of green corn plants creep right up to the city limits. A large plaque in the town square commemorates the Lincoln-Douglas debate that got held nearby. From the surface, in high relief, protrudes the toe of one of Mr. Douglas's boots. Years ago a commercial traveler from the South, or so local legend-mongers insist, paid black shoeshine boys to keep that boot free of the verdigris which—everyone has to agree—certainly has disfigured the face of Mr. Lincoln.

The Quincy of historical fact, the Quincy of inherited belief: they coexist, however grudgingly. But my volumes of folklore let me glimpse a certain entirety, one that I'm sure few other natives ever have seen. When I was growing up, everybody knew some of the entries I now spend hours reading. But no single person, of course, would have known all these variations; before the collectors copied them down, nobody ever had seen all of the county's beliefs assembled. In fact, by transcribing the entirety of Adams County's belief, the folklorists allow me to sense what is by implication a whole other world. Beginning with the Quincy of inherited belief, I've begun guessing my way outward, in all four directions. Sometimes I just know the whole planet lies wrapped in an atmosphere of belief, a dimension that is transparent, yet marked by its own currents, its own prevailing boundaries.

A lot of the folklorists' informants insisted that they themselves no longer subscribed to the beliefs they were describing. Interviewed at a time by now some twenty-five to fifty years in the past, they preferred to attribute their contributions to parents, or to grandparents. Other informants weren't sure: maybe they believed, and maybe not. But whether genuine or feigned, their skepticism only reminds us that belief admits of few firm edges. Even I, a vicarious believer at best, began these pages by noticing how it is that folk notions cling to my mind. Belief itself, like the flesh that we wear in folklore, amounts to a transition zone.

But what is the subtle attraction that folk beliefs hold for skeptics like me? Consider the two versions of Quincy which I mentioned above, that of historical fact, and that of inherited belief. If we live in the former—and surely we do, most of the time—why is it that the latter should keep impinging on our attention? Well, consider the fundamental difference between them. The landscape of fact remains coherent because of the primacy in it of cause and effect relations. Indeed the relation of cause and effect, according to the logic of fact, amounts to a counterpart in time to the spatial relation of figure and ground. On occasion, figure may reverse to ground, or cause to effect, but the degree to which such a reversal startles us only shows how fully the landscape of fact features stability.

In the landscape of belief, any element attracts or calls out to some other—to one with properties different from its own—in a self-effacing tendency that removes distinct boundaries from the attracting and the attracted alike. It's not that hair on the body makes one strong. Nor does strength cause hair to grow on us. Instead, a persistent correlation links the two properties; so the terms "cause" and "effect" become interchangeable, and therefore practically meaningless. The same correlation, obtaining between "figure" and "ground," is what permits the dying to appear across great distances, or lets a witch vanish before our eyes: in either case, the logic of belief implies, the image on which we focus becomes but another way of interpreting the periphery that frames it. So a minimal coherence characterizes the contours of belief. Sometimes, in fact, we can't see in belief anything at all like a "landscape." Sometimes it amounts to no more than a guarantee of dissonance, a promise of unpredictability.

Folk beliefs interrelate more by the rules of art than by those of conventional reality. Indeed such beliefs, viewed from a larger perspective, seem a kind of communal, ongoing artwork. People like me sense in them a collective project in which we participate, as in the raising of a cathedral, or a pyramid. Our individual participation remains so constant, however, that it turns transparent before us. To notice ourselves in the act of furthering a bit of folklore, we need to train a peculiar kind of attention on our own behavior, rather like what we have to do to catch ourselves in the act of blinking. In nailing a horseshoe above my garage door, I may not bring luck to my life, but I do insinuate into the minds of my children and my neighbors—if only indirectly—the ancient belief that the muscular, whinnying spirits of wind demand to be acknowledged.

We honor folk notions. But not because we believe in them. No, folk notions represent our collective, half-conscious effort to vivify the drab dailiness of our existence: they have a way of intensifying, of making more thrilling whatever regularity we count on in order to plan our lives. So the horseshoe relieves, however slightly, my weariness at the mechanical predictability by means of which I travel. And yet, what is the regularity from which folk beliefs offer to free us? Isn't it exactly that stability which lets us plan our lives? The very regularity of cause and effect relations nurtures us, even while it bores us. A cat struck by lightning is anything but stable.

The landscape of belief and that of fact are not opposed, or not diametrically, at least. No, they lie at some oblique angle to each other. Tired of the predictabilities that nourish, we long for that other world, the one we keep extrapolating, collectively, from scraps of belief. The landscape of belief relates to that of fact in rather the way the planet Pluto related, once, to Neptune. The orbit of the latter, or certain irregularities in it, let astronomers infer both the existence and location of a presence they'd never seen. They calculated awhile. And then aimed their telescopes in just the right direction to discover a planet, our ninth, the most obscure.

The older I get, the more folk beliefs stick in my mind. They arrange themselves all around the periphery of my thinking. I admire how they hover between life and art, these quirky, archaic forms of behavior. I admire how they tease my thinking out of its regular orbit. They infiltrate whatever I write, even unrelated topics, as if I'd tied a rabbit's foot to my computer keyboard.

We do dwell in the landscape of fact. But we never escape the tug a certain counterpart to it exerts. The attraction between the two reminds us that much of what we long for—invisible and stubborn though it is—does not sustain life.

FINDING
OUR LIVES

One February nearly ten years ago, I got invited to make a peyote pilgrimage. The Huichol Indians, of west central Mexico —with one of whom I was teaching at the time—maintain what many scholars call the most consistently pre-European world view in all North America. My colleague's name is Julio. To middle-class students born a bit late for the sixties, he taught weaving and that kind of painting, with colored yarns pressed into beeswax-coated plywood, by which the Huichols are represented in major museums. He invited several of us: the American professor of art history who had hired him, the Mexican architecture student who interpreted his Spanish to English, the interpreter's girlfriend. But why me? I really never knew. I recently had taught a course in what were then the four books of Carlos Castaneda, about an apprenticeship with don Juan Matus, a Yaqui *peyotero* from Sonora. Julio may have thought this a signal. Or he may have known I was a writer.

What happens during the peyote pilgrimage, or *peregrinación,* has been as patiently studied as Huichol art itself. Anthropologists and lay folk alike have puzzled over the eerie orthodoxy of these *peyoteros* who, unable to read or write, most of them, living in villages high in the sierra, or in slums at the edge of crowded Mexican cities, have walked for untold generations now to praise the same gods in the same remote desert valley in San Luis Potosí. And around the *peregrinación* centers practically all of Huichol culture, a way of life, in the words of anthropologist Peter T. Furst, "doubly precious because it is resilient enough to accommodate change without surrendering its vital center or even its external forms, and because it remains so unmistakably—even flagrantly—native American."

Returning from the *peregrinación,* I began at once to read what I could about it. I wanted to set what had happened in context. But something wouldn't budge. Some quality of those days in the desert didn't fit what I was finding, page by page, to be the general consensus of patient, humane anthropological observation. I particularly admired the work of Barbara Meyerhoff. Almost alone among students of the subject, she had what Julio would call "la presencia"—a subtlety keen enough to feel when she but half understood the situation before her. What did it mean, she asked don Ramón, of the vision she underwent the first time she ate peyote. That she quotes his reply shows why he must have admired her: "It means itself—nothing more!" However, that she then explains his remark is what lends, I finally felt, a tinny note to the discipline she so eloquently practices. Anthropology is an effort at completely literal speech. Rather than speaking directly to or of the gods, and in the ways they might demand, the anthropologist would make a composite of others' remarks and deeds—all in an effort to identify the ritual, the ideal form of it, and individual variations therefrom. But as the *peyoteros* love to point out, with a small smile—"We don't all say the same thing."

I never asked the meaning of what had happened to me. Lord knows, I had foolish questions enough. But not that one. Rather, I wanted to know what I should do. A certain luminous quality now held those days in the desert—held them before me, somehow—could I one day return? Would he take me again? Julio thought for a long time, when I asked. Then he wanted to know, and closely, what had happened.

Yes, he said finally, you may learn all about it, if you decide to. He went on to describe certain rules, or ways of living, that had mainly to do with diet and avoiding extramarital sex. It seemed that, after five journeys into the desert, I might even become a *mara'akame,* the singer who heals by being in touch with the gods. And so there came one night when I had to decide. As a chilly wind ran through the *huizache* plants, I felt completely foolish. I huddled there, self-conscious and cold. Over a small camp fire, Julio seemed to go on and on. A *peyotero* had, above all, to be sorry for his sins, *sus pecados.* And the main *pecado* was extramarital sex. We were here in the desert to weep like coyotes for our sins. Was I truly sorry?

We had already tied in a length of twine a knot for each of the people with whom, unmarried, we'd ever made love. Then he had burned the twine. And now it was bits of ash blown— who knows where—in the desert. Yes, I said finally, I am sorry. And right then, so help me, that very moment, a couple of coyotes on a ridge a mile or so away began yapping. I must have flinched with surprise.

Are you sure? he asked softly. Because they say you're lying. Now I thought hard. Were we saying the same thing, he and I?

Was I only deceiving myself? And worse, out of some dim desire to please? With all respect to them, I said, stubbornly, I think I truly am sorry.

And suddenly onto his face came that small smile. Don't waste your respect on them, ol' buddy. Everyone knows they're terrible liars.

The pilgrimage itself had begun with a bus ride of some six or eight hours to San Luis Potosí. From there, a train carried us through desert broken only by glimpses of towns, a hundred or so in population, of half-fallen adobe, or of chickens swaggering down an alley. Four teenage soldiers sprawled in adjoining seats, nodding over their comic books and M-16's. The sunlight bore down with a grip that left me catching my breath, as we climbed off the second-class car, into a town that seemed no different from twenty others we had passed. A crowd had gathered, not of course to greet us, but rather because the train represented the main variety in a day filled with gossip and watching pigs panting in a doorway. Elderly men and women eyed us warily. Julio and his cousin, also named Julio, wore the loose white cotton trousers and blouses, brimming with embroidered figures, that make the Huichol *peyotero* resemble no one else in all of Mexico. When the two of them approached, the crowd parted. The rest of us followed in silence.

With the mestizos, who represent some 80 percent of Mexico's population, the Huichols get along not at all. At various stages of our journey, now on foot, we would leave offerings to acknowledge some deed the gods had performed long ago at that very spot, often enough before men had ever existed. All the while, the Huichols would accuse the mestizos, sometimes under the breath, often aloud, and shrilly, of stealing these little gifts. The holiest of places lay, after all, but a brief walk from several villages. A ceremonial arrow, a fragment of gourd, a tiny mirror—any such offering might, like our locomotive and battered cars, provide some bored mestizo a moment's relief. At any rate, we left our offerings. We knew they'd be gone in the morning.

In the valley where we stood now, peyote grows and is gathered. The Huichols, native to a coastal range two hundred miles west, refer to this small dusky-green cactus as a deer, *nuestro venadito*. Anthropologists have puzzled at some length over this turn of phrase. It may be because the *peyoteros,* while making their pilgrimage, prefer to call all things by other names. Thus, a truck driver who offers a ride may become "our legs." The *peyotero* will often refer to his hat as "huaraches," the automobile-tire sandals that carry him through the desert. That the deer is further associated with corn—the stalk breaks through the ground like little horns, says Julio—may also have to do with it. But my own suggestion is simpler: peyote is quite difficult to see. It extends no more than an inch above the ground. Locate a plant but two or three steps away, then move your eye for an instant. You can keep looking for hours.

Everyone wants to hear about the peyote vision one undergoes there in the desert. Yet such curiosity is merely another kind of reductionism. What did you see when you ate the stuff? The question betrays a desire to strip away what are thought to be all the nonessential elements: the day or two of fasting before, the nights without sleep, the endless chanting and walking. The question is deeply naive. It has about it the greed or impatience of a small child. Even to call the experience a "vision" reveals, indirectly, how Euro-America overvalues the visual. I learned as much or more from my ears and fingertips, in those few hours. Yet somehow the question won't be turned away. What is that experience? How does it feel to be what they call *empeyotado?*

Well, the experience itself feels rather like writing these pages about it. Time slips from any framework. As I write this paragraph, for example (or one version of it anyway), I sit in a beach hotel in Mexico overlooking the sea. A breeze comes all day long off the water, bearing now and then an odor of dead fish or, fainter, under it all somehow, the odor of salt. Evenings, the breeze runs from land to sea. I can smell flowers, the asphalt someone is pouring farther inland. I know certain of the sentences passing now below my hand may not be quite right. But no matter. I'll fix them in a week, or in a year. I can return at will to this page. Indeed, I have, in a way, been here before. Was I not here a month ago, three thousand miles north, pondering how I could ever explain to you the effect of eating peyote? A lift-off into simultaneity, I decided I would tell you— that was the main feature. It was less of a lie than, well, the alternatives. Yet, I know tomorrow I'll turn all dissatisfied. I'll try to tell you that men and women walk into the valley because from there they can see farther in all directions. I'll want you to know that one time, walking out after days there, dizzy with thirst, I thought sure we'd all die. What did I see then? Only five men walking through the desert. Though I knew that everything else in my life, after that moment, would feel like a dream. Tomorrow, I'll probably want you to know all that.

Consider it another way. In overemphasizing the psycho-chemical effects of the cactus, people presume to know exactly when it was the *peyotero*'s vision started. Just as they ignore the deeper implication: the very truest vision has no end.

Professor Meyerhoff, in her book on the *peregrinación*, mentions briefly how over the years she has come to understand more and more of what happened to her. The burden of literal speech precludes her discussing in any detail her breakthroughs in understanding. But I feel I know what she means. I have stopped, right in the crosswalk of a busy street, nearly getting run over, so powerful was the sudden fitting of an image, or turn of phrase, into some context already ten years old. It always bears the feel of details yielding a heretofore hidden coherence. And the number of details grows to be immense because, quite simply, you are told to memorize all that happens on the pilgrimage: the names given those who accompany you, the words to the endless prayers, the sequence of offerings, as well as, hour by hour, the exact conditions of wind, light, weather, the number and kinds of birds, and where they flew, the reptile and insect life.

Demands on your attention have begun somewhere during the journey, well before that point when, mind empty as you can make it, flanked by people now intimate to you, you walk in complete silence for hours, eyes scanning the desert floor. The forms of life around you, like different points on the land itself, figure in the songs and talk you've been hearing for days, if not for all your life. The spider bears a particular value, rather like that of a musical note. The owl bears another. If it should rain, all beneficent aspects get intensified. So the landscape finally becomes a shifting text. Its syntax is not always clear. And I myself know but a little of the vocabulary. Still, a reading of any day there comes to be possible, indeed inevitable. A man's first reading may be wrong, of course. It may be more a comment on him than on that moment. And any given image of course may take years to resolve. So it happens that Professor Meyerhoff, *peyotera* that she is, continues years after, with her eyes to the ground.

The above comparison—landscape as text—represents my reading of something that happened the first time we hunted peyote. I have returned more than once; and in other ways, like Professor Meyerhoff, I never leave. But this event felt very much like a signal. Let me try to say it as literally as possible.

We had walked for many hours, and found not a single peyote plant. We were tired and discouraged, though no one spoke. (So how did I know we all were discouraged? The intimacy is relentless. You believe those about you know your least thought. You even blank your mind to avoid distracting them.) Now we sat on a boulder on a little rise, light-headed, tongues swollen from thirst. Everyone waited for Julio to do something. Fifteen or twenty minutes went by. Then out of nowhere, down a hill drifted a lone whirlwind, twenty or so feet in height. It crossed in front of us. It went off down the valley floor into shadow. Julio stood up abruptly, and said we had to follow it. We did. And we found, within a quarter-mile, on ground I was sure we already had covered, hundreds of little green peyotes.

In the weeks that followed, in Guadalajara, and later in the United States, I began noticing that shape, the peculiar whirling helix form of the wind that had guided us. In airports, for no apparent reason, I would suddenly realize that propellers were leaving that shape in the air, if I could only see it. Or I'd catch myself watching the water twirl from a sink or a bathtub. I began to think I saw such a shape hovering over a friend's head, or gone down a highway, and even beckoning, once, at a cliff's edge. I didn't care at all what they meant. I wondered what I should do. Julio, when I asked him, thought just a moment and said, talk to them. When I did, and learned to listen, with mind blank, to what then entered my mind, I began to arrive. Landscape remains a language we only half understand.

There remains, of course, the chance that Julio tricked us.

Maybe he knew those plants were there. Yet, anyone who knows the *peyoteros* would find that objection ludicrous. They are too serious for theatrics. They are too serious even to be somber. But, suppose it. Suppose with the cynic—who lives in terror at the prospect, and so is half-convinced already, of the shaman's unearthly power—suppose we were tricked. I am then left with what? A much subtler sense of landscape than I had before. And one I can't imagine having learned any other way. Yet, but, see here now—the cynic's objection hovers before us. Apparently, it won't go away. We had better talk to it.

Sincerity has become the issue. The languages of Europe—and what are they but the home of the social sciences?—Spanish and English, in this case, both want to know only the facts. These languages long ago began somehow, in one degree or another, to mistrust their own metaphors. They now rather prefer—as only languages could—a perfectly literal speech. Men trained as social scientists run the governments of countries in which these tongues are official. And those of us who dwell in them tend to worry about the truth or falsehood of a remark more than about its author's sincerity. Yet, by just that much, we misunderstand the *peyotero*. For him, truth and falsehood remain but a crude binary representation of things. Like the camp fire over which he begs forgiveness for feelings he knows he couldn't help having, the *peyotero* listens for sincerity alone; he pursues it in his deeds and in his words. Yet his is not the sincerity of Hallmark Cards, or presidential messages. That we might think so only shows how deeply we lack the concept.

Sincerity, for the *peyotero,* involves knowing all of the context in which he is about to act. He listens to himself, as well as to you, as carefully as he notices the direction of the wind, and of the birds. He seems laconic because to explain overmuch—to connect the images too often—would be to imply you're not paying attention. But if you're not, what are you doing here, days from home, thirsty and exhausted in a desert valley? So, the *peyotero* shows us the self-deception behind any lack of sincerity.

Because, like Professor Meyerhoff, he puzzles at them lovingly, the details of his days in the desert knit one another ever more clearly in place for the *peyotero*. That time begins to feel like the present tense to him, it so benchmarks all other days of his life. From there, in those days, he begins to believe he can feel the future. His sincerity turns to a form of augury. And so he reminds us that even European languages, for two thousand years, have connected both augury and authority with the authentic.

But I am an author. I am trying to tell as clearly as I can of my relationship with a man vastly my superior. He is not so by birth, but by culture: his gods have made him kind, funny, durable. More than anyone else I have met, he forever knows exactly where he is. I call that intelligence: a sensitivity to the ratios that hold us in the world. Exactly my own age, ironically enough, he works when he can at odd jobs, or goes about selling yarn paintings, to feed his wife and four children. I suppose you might consider him merely another painter. Though once he confided to me how ludicrous it felt to teach yarn painting to youngsters who never hunted peyote. Another four of his children have died in infancy. He has no permanent address.

However often you make the pilgrimage to that valley, one rule remains in effect. No *peyotero* may live there. Anthropologists always get told some grave illness would find the man who sought to remain. I think I know why. It is because the hour by hour suffering brought by the journey would be diminished. The *peyoteros* always say they go there to find their life, *para encontrar nuestra vida*. Peyote, after all, can be bought in downtown market stalls. But only of plants acquired by someone having patiently suffered the heat and cold, the hunger and thirst and exhaustion—only of these is the *peyotero* confident. Every time he arrives in that valley, or usually anyway, he weeps.

MONUMENT

We drive for an hour with a black crystalline wall, two hundred feet high, inches from one fender. Then we cross a rise. And blink at a whole lakeful of that brackish, alkaline water that cripples used to swear restored mobility to their limbs. Now the road swings east, then north, to where a body of deeper water jiggles, wide, blue: Banks Lake lies tucked into what was once the biggest canyon of all. Grand Coulee, people called the mile-deep crevice that lay here, fifty years ago. When the government built the dam of the same name across the Columbia, river water backed up, diverted, and filled the whole thing.

It's a warm June night when we pull into the town of Grand Coulee. We arrive just in time to get to the dam, to watch the U.S. Bureau of Reclamation's new laser light show. We huddle below a wall 350 feet high, the concrete of it pressing the river back into spillways, in Canada, four hundred miles north. From a control booth overhead, the Bureau projects figures against the concrete. From loudspeakers a voice, huge, otherworldly, accompanies the hiss and spit of colored light. *I am power,* it intones, *I was here when floods scoured channels and canyons into volcanic rock. I am the river. I am power.*

Image by image, The Voice's tone takes on the contrived breathlessness of a porno movie. Vibrant with intimacy, it hints that the dam lets us exercise control over what amounts to the landscape's rich, passive body: converting the river's weight into electrical power, irrigating windy dust till it blooms with orchards, wheat fields.

The Bureau's presentation amounts to a kind of commercial for the Bureau, my wife whispers. And she's right. In three or four minutes The Voice describes the entire geological history of the area. All of native Americans' time here gets described in forty-five seconds. Ninety seconds suffice for characterizing Euro-American pioneers. Then, for an hour, The Voice lingers over quantifiable details of the dam: its 12 million cubic yards make this the largest concrete structure ever built, a shape 5,673 feet in length, rising 550 feet above the old riverbed. Through all eleven of the drum gates, each 135 feet long, a million cubic feet of water a second are able to spill. Eight and one-half miles of inspection galleries honeycomb the structure, and two and a half miles of shafts.

A certain assumption runs through all that's said, monotonous as the synthesizer disco music in the background: before the Bureau happened along, the river's power was wasted, if not destructive. But now, The Voice makes it clear, the river's become a useful and productive citizen of the area. When we look around, we see that most of the crowd, parked at curbside, watches from RV's that bear out-of-state plates. A few families slump on benches, the kids nodding off clutching teddy bears and blankets, fathers and mothers training their glazed eyes on the concrete wall.

The next morning, we wake stiff from a sagging motel mattress. The proprietress, chatting over coffee, tells us a Japanese engineer stayed for seven years in the room we occupy. He was here to help install computer parts, she thinks, in the third power plant, in the early sixties. An actress, she herself grew up here and left, returning only a year ago, when her mother died of cancer and left her the business. Like those on either side of it, her motel has flourished and withered, over the years, in the grip of the boom-bust economy the dam provides the town. Every decade for the last half-century, a different project has brought in new payrolls: the workers stay for maybe six or eight years, then leave. Our hostess says she plans to convert some of her units into a laundromat, or maybe into a convenience store. Outside her door, salmon-colored paint flakes from the cinder-block walls onto the sidewalk.

In chilly morning air, we prowl the streets and alleys. The buildings date from the forties and fifties: before the dam got built, no town existed here. To canyon walls steep as sights on a rifle, bait shops and restaurants cling, hotels and fast-food joints, businesses aimed at the tenuous tourism that keeps the town alive between the Bureau's budget binges. And then, when we turn a corner, the dam looms huge and white, the mile-long gleam of it binding one canyon wall to the other. When we blink, a trick of perspective ripples through us. We focus on the tiny dots crossing at the top, and then remind ourselves that they are trucks.

But we're here to look at something else. On the canyon slope opposite the one our motel occupies, we walk the length of B Street, once the main drag of the boom town that was home to the thousands of workers who built the dam, from 1933 to 1939. Vacant lots gape, block after block. Twenty or so deserted house trailers huddle on a corner, half their windows broken out, a door swinging open. Holes twenty feet deep yawn in many lots. The first time I saw them, I compared those holes to bomb craters, the area's so desolate, the sagebrush and the blue sky crowd in so. But no, they're only cellars dug below some of the several hundred wooden buildings that stood here. We carry copies of old photos and even a list, drawn up by some old-timer, of the businesses that flourished here. We wander up and down the broken sidewalks, orienting ourselves with fuzzy black and white snapshots.

We'd give anything, we decide, to know where Harry Wong's Chinese Noodle Parlor stood, or Sam Bernstein's Clothing Store, or the Hod Carrier's Hall. In all this bare dirt, isn't there room for so much as a single roofing nail from the Peerless Painless Dentists, or the Best Little Store by a Damsite? Marching back and forth we recite, like the punch line of some joke, the names of places a person once could choose to spend the night: the Columbia Club Hotel, or maybe the Deluxe or the Star, the Bungalow or the Bigalow or the Bickle, Baker's Cabins or those of Al Roberts, the Seattle Rooming House or the Frontier. We wish we'd got here fifty years ago, in time for breakfast at the Wagon Wheel, or to grab lunch from the Hot Tamale Man, and to stop for a cone at Babe Hopkins's Ice Cream Shop. Except for walking to work at the project site, a person never needed to leave these blocks.

Only the Grand Coulee Club remains, a long, narrow building of one story, behind which the hillside plunges at such an angle the basement windows, toward the back, lie exposed. The door's boarded shut, with a sign warning the whole structure might collapse at any minute. So we peer in through the front windows at the dance floor, noses pressed to the dusty glass. Feet planted exactly where children must have stood to ogle the taxi dancers, we squint at the murky interior.

By now the official litanies of kilovolts and acre feet bore us. Instead, we're attracted to the utter ordinariness of those who dug and poured, who brought the whole thing off, payday after payday. Who cares how much water and power the project provides? We want to hear more, for example, about all the unemployed masons the contractor had to find and hire: the inspectors discovered, after awhile, that only fellows skilled at working gravestones could finish the river's granite floor smooth enough for the concrete to grip. And yet, it was the very kind of thinking on display last night at the light show that administered this project, and kept the records. It was the mind's power of quantification, worshiped with a near-religious intensity, that turned columns of figures into columns of concrete. What gets us, in particular, is how the official version of the dam's construction seems to ignore B Street. Down among all those switchyards, under the five-inch cables, in the middle of plaques and reports and display cases, only a scrapbook of photos tucked away in the Visitors Center—without a single name attached, by the way—admits that specific individuals blasted the rock and mixed the concrete, slept and ate in the buildings that lined these vacant lots.

One kind of power certainly does get generated hereabouts by holding back four hundred miles of water. But another, very different kind of power comes from all this failure to acknowledge what is a very recent, very human past. Sleek, massive, and impersonal, the dam by now for us begins to represent the anonymity of those who built it. It amounts to a memorial, one far more moving in fact than any the Bureau would have subsidized. Yes, we agree, it's a lot better than some idealized sculpture of The Worker would have been. We consider it a monument. We even remember how the same Latin root yields both *monument* and *monster:* the two terms have in common the notion of issuing a warning, a reminder. Because for us the dam is both a reminder and a warning.

And yet it takes a fair amount of time to find someone who actually remembers the dam being built. Finally we knock on the trailer door of Ida B., the octogenarian widow recommended by our motel owner. Barely five feet tall, she walks with a cane. And a cataract has cost her the sight in one eye. But her conversation dips and soars like the landscape out her window. She recalls the day, right at the start of excavation, when she noticed smoke rising from the top of a river-bank cave, and a stovepipe jutting out. Approaching the mouth, she eased back the army blanket strung across the front, to discover inside a woman nursing a baby. The floor was covered with straw. A couple of apple crates, and a wood stove, amounted to the only furnishings. Would the gentleman of the house be back soon? she asked. Sartenly not, the woman replied in a thick Missouri twang—not till his shift at the dam site gits over.

Probably because Ida's late husband was a union secretary, she recalls the dam as an exercise in grass-roots political organization. She remembers the story of Billy Clapp sitting over coffee in an Ephrata restaurant, when he suddenly figured out how to irrigate the miles of sagebrush hills that he and his friends inhabited: to raise water from the river, five hundred feet below, they needed to build a dam that'd use the big coulee as reservoir. She recalls Jim O'Sullivan agitating for the project, struggling for twenty years against the private power companies' accusation of "socialism." She recalls the visits of FDR, the ham sandwiches he ate. His wheelchair still stands in a glass case in the Visitors Center. But she doesn't like to talk about B Street. Times were hard, and the streetwalkers were poor. They did what they had to. What would we have done? she wants to know.

Except for the memories of people Ida's age, a few pages of news writing now half a century old provide the only surviving accounts of the men who built the dam. The feeding and housing of thousands of workers, out in the middle of the desert, apparently made for entertaining reading. The *Nation*, in 1935, sent a reporter who found little in the town but "squalor and cupidity." It seemed built, he wrote, of "faith, hope, barn siding and paper board." Its fifteen hundred inhabitants enjoyed "twenty eating places, as many saloons, at least a half-dozen wide-open brothels, five grocery stores, two jewelry stores, a furniture store, two drugstores, three ladies' wear shoppes, three beauty shoppes, . . . and six real-estate agents." We almost can feel our journalist shaking his head, at how fast money multiplies out here: he describes a speculator turning down $2,250 for a corner lot of the same sticky desert mud that had cost him a dollar an acre, three years earlier. In and out of the reportage wander ladies of the evening, walking ankle deep in mud, on their way to visit the hairdresser.

By 1937, the atmosphere has changed. Or at least reporters' expectations have. A writer from *Harper's* notices news photos of FDR thumbtacked on rooming-house walls. The older workers are veterans of Boulder Dam, on the Colorado; the younger fellows wear letter sweaters from nearby universities. On the highways leading into town from the east and south, rusted trucks and jalopies appear and vanish, their license plates from Kansas or Nebraska or Dakota, bedsprings and quilts and brooms tucked in the trailers they tow. From one of them a fellow flashes a roll of five-dollar bills bound with a rubber band.

But it's from the pages of the *Wenatchee World* that we get what most nearly resembles a day-by-day account of the workers' lives. The nearest town of any size—although known, before the project, mainly for its apple orchards—Wenatchee took an understandable pride in all the attention the dam brought the area. Rufus Woods, editor of the *World,* a long-time lobbyist for the dam, soon devoted a weekly news page to it.

Right from the start, the demand for work exceeded the number of jobs. In January 1934, Col. Carl Beery, contact for the National Reemployment Service, has to ask the *World* for help "in keeping would-be workers from the damsite." And yet G. A. Sellar, of Sellar Realty, promises to provide housing for "workmen with families, who wish to be in quiet, home-like surroundings." Within days Beery announces no more employment figures will be given, as each set prompts a mob to gather, seeking work.

The *World* describes the newborn town of Grand Coulee as amounting to twenty or thirty buildings, acrid exhaust fumes rising off the mud-gumbo streets, a drugstore perched on the canyon's edge, and a school with seventeen pupils and five books. The residents exude a certain friendliness, many of them recognizing each other from earlier projects. The *World* decides that what they're doing resembles "pioneering." It compares their morale to the spirit of Poker Flat.

Sidewalks appear, then graveled streets, then a weekly newspaper. By the end of February, mail's arriving. The first few weeks of March see taxi, shoeshine, and soda-fountain service. Before long, the first movie's shown. But many men apparently never found Mr. Sellar's bucolic ideal, the placid work place at the edge of which a fellow supplied most of his own needs with "a cow, chickens and a garden." By the end of March, two Nespelem Indians drown while stringing phone wire across the river. (The *World* remembers that Wilson Joe was "an excellent basketball player." His colleague, Anton Frances, "had a liberal education.") Some months later Ben Butterton loses a hand to a cement mixer. And E. A. Brown goes to bed in perfect health, and never awakes. (Brown was a roommate of Tex Owens, killed a month earlier when a piece of dynamite cap blew through his heart.) When a 120-foot crane boom falls on Marvin Palenuk, a pile driver, he suffers a cut head, two broken arms, and a broken leg. Rescuers have to dig below the boom and cut it with torches to free him.

And yet, if they aren't getting hurt or killed, the *World* scarcely notices individual workers. It prefers, instead, to quantify their existence. It quotes with satisfaction, for example, the 1937 safety engineer's report about having in stock 2,430 hard hats, as well as 923 safety belts, 234 respirators, 1,012 clear-lens goggles (not to mention 408 goggles of other types), 396 vests, 48 ring life preservers and 1,200 pounds of protective cream for concrete workers. In 1939, the *World* notes that, since construction began, money orders worth nearly 5 million dollars have been sent out of the area. To every college library in the country, Major S. E. Hutton, assistant director of the Bureau's Information Department, is mailing a booklet entitled *Grand*

Coulee Dam. But surely not one of the fifty pages, and not a single one of the hundred pictures, ever acknowledged the existence, at the site, of anything like the blasphemies and fist fights, the whiskey and tobacco spit that we figure surely existed.

Whether they came from Wenatchee or New York, the tone of the writers who covered the project betrayed a certain self-congratulatory optimism. They'd managed, after all, to convince themselves that the future would share their feelings about the heroic, history-wrenching effects of building the dam. But from the perspective of today, a mere fifty years into that future, their optimism sounds a little tinny. The dam didn't provide irrigated small farms for thousands of poor families. It did make electrical power cheaper, and more plentiful; and by powering aluminum plants in the Pacific Northwest, the dam may have won the Second World War, in the bargain. But equally productive dams have grown up around it. And lately nuclear plants have threatened to provide an even cheaper, if more deadly, source of power.

Far from seeming to us the heroic achievement that the journalists thought it would, the dam has begun already to recede, and not just into history, but also into the landscape. Right from the start, the riverbed required regular dredging—to keep its silt from building up, turning the dam to nothing more than another waterfall, on a river that always has created waterfalls. Of course not even Billy Clapp, gazing over his coffee cup, thought the thing would last forever. It always has needed upkeep. But every little sign of wear, and every replacement part it requires, does manage, after all, to throw into sharper relief the dam's twin features: that of reminding us of its builders, even as it warns us about ourselves.

It warns us that yes, we can light our homes, and turn the desert fertile, but at a terrible cost. In order to exercise such power over our surroundings, we need to train on ourselves the same quantifying gaze that we aim at the nonhuman world we want to control. We have to consider ourselves, or people very much like us, to be no more than the units that measure them.

And yet the dam reminds us that we have another, very different kind of power as well: we can intuit what it must have felt like to live, for awhile, on B Street. If we remember the mix of feelings we have entertained about our own work, we can extrapolate what sort of emotions would've run through those workers of whom we know, by now, so very little. The dam, in short, reminds us that we need to imagine those who built it. Their irreverence, a kind of restless glee—not to mention their healthy disrespect for all authority—has to have made it hard for middle-class journalists to describe them. Most of the work force, I tell my wife, probably would have resembled my buddy Yukon John Tomsich.

A mutual friend, years ago, introduced me to John. The two of them had met when John was hitchhiking into a town fifty miles south of here, from the desert shack he was living in at the time. A big, nondescript dog trailed at his heels. John allowed as how he was going into town for drinking water. Himself, he'd as soon drink out of the irrigation ditch, but he was pretty sure it'd kill the dog. Within weeks John had gone to work driving a cat for my friend's construction outfit. He said he didn't want pay. He'd trade his time for the twenty-year-old Cadillac sedan in my friend's back yard. Before long the car was running, and John was living in it. By August he'd driven it into the hills, and poached himself an elk. The air conditioning, turned on high, worked just dandy for keeping all that meat chilled and fresh. By October, John had another plan. He had bought a couple of piglets, and was raising them in the Cadillac's trunk. Figured he could fatten them on persimmons. (He'd got a real good deal on a couple of dozen bushels.) We'd all have persimmon-finished pig for Thanksgiving.

Maybe because he'd put in so many years traveling, John preferred to spend his free time planted in the nearest saloon, knocking back beer after beer, pulling on the Pall Mall cigarette forever dangling out of his long black beard, rocking back and forth on his bar stool, crooning "Let's get drunk and beeee somebody." Had Yukon John ever, in fact, worked at Grand Coulee Dam? Well, after so many miles, he needed to be a bit vague about a lot of the details. He'd started out mining uranium, back in Utah. His wife had been a fine Mormon lady. So when she and the neighbor fellow cheated him out of a claim he'd staked, and then he found he'd got the black lung, but couldn't get a single government pension—why, he flat hit the road. A guy had to be willing to work at anything. Take one time he was broke, and had to help set up the tents for a circus. He happened to lean up against the gorilla's cage, to catch his breath. Well the gorilla didn't do a damn thing but reach through the bars, and grab John's wrist, right like that, and commence to squeezing. John didn't know what to do. So with his free hand, he grabbed the *gorilla's* wrist, and started squeezing right back. They kept at it, the two of them, staring each other in the eye, for ten minutes or so. Damned if they both didn't let go at the same time.

I haven't seen John in years. But my wife always gets a kick out of hearing stories about him. In fact she and I are talking about him as we drive out of Grand Coulee. We're talking about the kind of attachment people like John must've felt to the shanty town that huddled, once, in the sagebrush back on those hills. Everybody knew the job couldn't last forever. A fellow would work for a couple of months, then drift off to try his luck elsewhere, only to return broke and sheepish. They moved about so much their lives must've felt like the country around them, an unbroken series of interruptions, one perspective unfolding, yielding another. Probably they were descended from generations of wanderers. Certainly they came from every state then in the Union, the kind of men and women who wind up leaving their kids only a faint, hangdog loyalty to a place, or a series of places. The children grow up to possess, like their parents, no more than the thinnest sense of belonging, of being part of a larger group of people.

A generation removed from the Great Depression, my wife and I are old enough that our fathers could have worked here for awhile. Neither of them did, in fact. But maybe it just never occurred to them. Anyhow, they certainly were a couple of good old boys who lived to travel. A footloose construction worker, her dad kept employed in ways that had my wife attending thirty-two schools before junior high. I grew up as the bored, carsick son of a salesman hustling, while he was young, from one territory to another. Here and there across the western United States, when we were children, our families paused. She recalls when a windstorm blew a frozen spruce limb smack through the roof of their house trailer. During what still seems like that year-long afternoon we put in crossing Death Valley, I recall standing at road side, peeing, while a buzzard circles overhead, and then pukes on the hood of our car.

Within the last two years, though only in their midseventies, both of our fathers have died. After shuddering through a series of strokes, hers fought to sit up, staring as if he'd just arrived and were noticing, for the first time, the tubes and needles and oxygen tanks all around him. Drowning in the carbon dioxide his lung cancer filled him with, mine managed a smile across whatever distance it was he could feel, when the nurse showed my sister that she had to shout for him to hear.

Neither of our fathers was born out here in the West. And yet each was a creature, like the dam itself, of intermontane North America, this stretch of desert that has provided—to no one knows how many generations—one excuse after another for wandering up and down it. Whether real-estate developers or hunter-gatherers, people who live here opt for a landscape that hovers somewhere between chance and willpower—pitiless as daylight on a Las Vegas casino, impersonal as a mushroom cloud above White Sands.

❊

Grand Coulee drops behind the horizon. As we head for where we live, three valleys away, the state road wanders in and out of sagebrush, cottonwood, bunchgrass. Wherever the soil stretches too thin, the underlying basalt bulges like a cheek-bone, or an elbow, revealing a black skeletal presence under the contours that we're crossing. Vivid, restless energy animates the landscape. Where the paths of long-vanished floods race back and forth, one gorge undercuts another, leaving an empty mouth hanging a couple of hundred feet in the air. At Dry Falls, a basin three and a quarter miles across drops, four hundred feet straight down, into different alcoves, pools of water on the bottom reflecting the sky.

ON THE
CONQUEST

Even the briefest visit to Mexico leaves the visitor dizzy with contradictions. As we cross that subway landing in the national capital, the one they've built around a prehispanic pyramid, right in front of our eyes, past and present struggle for mastery. No corner of the country remains isolated enough to be free of polarities. I remember twenty-some years ago, eyeing the nightly news, in a tiny town, on a dim TV screen. It fascinated me how a specially designed government railroad car was struggling to transport a huge stone statue of Tláloc—Aztec divinity of rain—through five hundred miles of jungle, to where it could be displayed outside the national museum. Because of the weather, the journey seemed to be taking forever. Record cloud bursts were following Tláloc, day after day, down those steel rails, on his way to his new temple.

It probably owes to the Conquest, this giddy feel that, wherever we go in Mexico, contraries of time or culture keep on getting mixed. It was the Conquest, probably, with its diverse points of view, its floating loyalties and shifting alliances, that lent the country its first and fiercest multiplicity. Mexico, to this day, recapitulates the shock waves let loose in those few months, when the two halves of the world, making contact, released an energy something like the impact that sperm and ovum have on each other. And yet by now, even to recount the Conquest to ourselves, we have to simplify it: we have to consider it a trajectory that resulted from the collision of two world views, that of the Spaniard and that of the Aztec.

The two outlooks with which we begin, like the documents on which we base them, agree on very little—maybe only on the fact that the Spaniards were so few, and the Aztecs, so many. Bernal Díaz, a foot soldier with Cortés, remembers that "We numbered five hundred and eight, not counting a hundred ship-masters, pilots, and sailors." Eleven ships and sixteen horses and mares, thirty-two crossbowmen and thirteen musketeers, a few bronze guns, four falconets, and a lot of powder and ball—for the Spanish king, it certainly didn't represent much of an investment. But that modest show of force soon was bringing to Spain more wealth than Spain had ever seen.

As early as the seventh day of July, in 1519—a little more than two months before Moctezuma and Cortés are to meet—the latter writes a letter to Carlos V. Its concluding paragraphs mention that His Majesty will receive, by messenger, a wheel of gold weighing 238 pounds, carved with the figures of mon-sters. Other gifts are also on the way: two necklaces of gold and rare stones, two pairs of leggings (one gold leaf and yellow deerskin, the other of white deerskin and silver leaf), a green-feathered bird with feet and beak and eyes of gold, the heads of two wolves and two tigers, two cotton sheets embroidered with figures in black and white, six brush paintings and two women's shirts. From our perspective, four centuries later, the splendor and variety of the gifts prefigure much of what the Aztec City of Tenochtitlán will offer. Cortés even includes six pounds of gold, that His Majesty may melt it, and see for himself its quality. The longer we ponder them, the more we begin to consider these first gifts as a kind of omen.

From the Aztec perspective, for many years before the Spaniards' arrival, omens had wrenched the landscape. In the *Codex Florentino*, Bernardino de Sahagún's Aztec informants tell of a flame shape that opened in the sky overhead: wide at the base and narrowing toward the top, like an ear of corn, it bled fire a drop at a time, as if the sky were wounded. When the people cried out, beating the palms of their hands against their mouths, they sounded like thousands of bells being shaken. All on its own, a temple burst into flames, wings of fire seeming to rush out the doors, to carry the walls off into the sky. Wind blew the lake into boiling, raging waves that lashed the walls of houses till they collapsed. Night after night, up and down the streets, people heard what sounded like a woman weeping, shouting to her children to flee the City, wondering where she should take them. At last fishermen netted a strange bird: it resembled a crane, except that it was the color of ashes and, in the crown of its head, bore a mirror which reflected, even at noon, the three stars to which the City burned incense every night.

It doesn't matter who's doing the talking. Whether we're listening to Spaniard or Aztec, the voices that ring within our story touch off, in each other, a kind of counterpoint. The deepest assumptions of the conquered manage to throw into relief those of the conqueror. Each lends, to whatever the other describes, a dizzying dimensionality. Whether from depths of wretchedness, or from heights of exhilaration, each perspective views the Conquest the way it does because of its definition of what comprises human existence.

The essence of the Spaniard is a soul, a sliver of existence both immortal and immaterial. The soul is also simple, seamlessly unified, indivisible into further components. But the nature of the Aztec is double: each is not just himself or herself, but is also a *nahualli*. At the moment of birth, each Aztec gets associated with a specific bit of plant or animal life, or maybe with a few inches of dirt, or a glimpse of sky. Each of the gods, even, is bound to this kind of other: to an owl or to an eagle, say, to a coyote or a coati. Sorcerers, those who practice magic, simply have learned to control these alternate selves, these exterior souls: shoot a bat, and you'll likely scar a witch. An arrow in a caiman leaves a *curandero* limping.

So Aztecs and their gods alike live subject to one rule: an element of otherness, an opposite number, balances each of them. As they watch the stars march across the sky, the Aztecs feel the year grind past with a mathematical regularity, a month at a time. They know that the very moment of the day on which the child is born fixes her future, predicts his potential. And yet, given all the balanced foreshadowing, given that the whole world's a network of anticipations, the *nahualli* lends to human experience an incomplete, disconnected quality.

Even Quetzalcóatl, Lord of the Air, when fetching back from the underworld all that was left of human ancestors, had to ask his *nahualli* how to revive their splintered bones. (He heard a voice say to bleed on them, bleed on them.) Aztecs can't conceive of existing alone, as only a self: the *nahualli*'s paw prints carry them all which directions; its root systems bind them to earth. Her *nahualli* can lend feathers to a woman, or sharp teeth; it frees her from the isolation of individuality. No wholeness can threaten the man whose *nahualli* roams the streets and paths of the Aztec Empire. Without *nahuallis* the earth would collapse into sameness.

The self and the *nahualli* amount to different versions of the same person: each is able to give the other advice, or to take the other's directions. And yet, though people born at the same moment share the same *nahualli*, each individual amounts to a different interpretation of it. The *nahualli* does predispose the self in certain ways, just as tomorrow predisposes today; like the future and the present, *nahualli* and self amount to paraphrases of each other.

Behind *nahualli* and soul, after all, lie two different concepts of time. The Spaniard understands time as linear and progres-

sive, as a series of moments possessing a plot—a sequence of
events flowing in one direction, interconnected by cause and
effect. The soul needs such a medium to survive, to refine itself.
Time, for the Spaniard, will come to an end at the moment
Christ returns to judge the souls of men and women. The Aztec,
on the other hand, understands time as gliding, circular and
endless, about the fixed axis of a ceremonial year. The individual
human is not immortal, or only minimally so. Of far greater im-
portance are the combinations, the endlessly recurring days on
which humans can get born into relation with a fixed, preexist-
ing number of *nahuallis*. This sense of time as repetition leaves
the Aztecs forever watching for omens, for moments which pre-
figure moments yet to come. The Spaniards' sense of time as
change leaves them measuring evidence, calculating, guessing.
The future, for the Aztec, not only is fixed, but also lies en-
coded in the natural world, in a kind of writing that people who
are learned in such matters can decipher. For the Spaniard the
future, at least in its particulars, remains largely indeterminate,
depending as it does on human choice.

And yet the Spaniards seem, at times, to know their deeds are
going to wind, forever after, through the imagination of Europe
and the Americas. When the islands through which they are
sailing start to yield signs of human life, to indicate that the
jungle overgrowing the mainland hides cities, they begin with a
special fervor to commend themselves to their God, and to the
future. And yet, ironically, the landscape first gives them back
reflections of lives exactly like their own, traces of the presence
of Spanish explorers, wanderers. Cortés's secretary, Lopéz de
Gómara, reports that when they catch a huge shark off Cozu-
mel, it carries in its belly three shoes, a cheese, a tin plate, and
ten flitches of salt pork. They even begin to run across Span-
ish castaways. One is named Guerrero. Having lived among the
natives so long by now that his face is tattooed, and both ear-

lobes bored, he refuses to leave. On the other hand Aguilar, a prisoner only eight years, limps into camp clutching an oar, rags at his waist, scraps of an old book of prayers tied in a bundle at one shoulder. He begs to come along as interpreter.

The first natives the Spaniards encounter seem nothing special. They certainly give no sign that, within weeks, they'll be collaborating with their conquerors to furnish the quasi-historical chronicle now unrolling before us. Indeed, the first natives take one look at the Spaniards and flee. Cortés and his men find only a temple full of fowls and idols, of toys and ornaments made of debased gold. Destroying the altar, pulling down the gods, Cortés cuts a limestone altar to the Virgin. These people live like filthy children, Bernal Díaz writes, or like gypsies. Each time the cannon fires, they shout, whistle, throw up straw and dust in the air, their faces painted, their limbs in quilted-cotton armor. Even though they've fled, the Spaniards suspect they'll be back. In fact, their numbers are so great that, if each only lifts a handful of dust, they'll bury this little band of adventurers. Cortés orders his men to dress the horses' wounds in fat cut from dead Indians.

By now it's begun to exhibit the resilience of a dialogue, the tale our sources are telling us. If, a moment ago, we heard the Spaniards' report of the first contacts, by now the Aztec version of the same events begins to reply. The Aztec authors of the *Crónica Mexicana* describe how, day by day, Moctezuma senses generations worth of prophecy solidifying, becoming rumor: the empire has been invaded. To verify the existence of the strange beings the rumors describe, he sends out scouts. But they keep coming back with their ears and toes cut off. The *Crónica* mentions the scouts catching glimpses of strangers, light skinned with long beards, dressed in blue or red, black or green jackets, wearing large round hats shaped like griddles. These fellows' hair reaches only to their ears. They're fishing. Moctezuma knows it must be Quetzalcóatl returning, just as he said he would, to end the world by wreaking revenge on certain other gods, in particular on those who drove him from this land. So Moctezuma sends messengers with gifts: a serpent (or *coatl*) mask inlaid with turquoise, a breastplate of *quetzal* feathers, a collar of reeds woven around a gold disk, a shield of gold and mother-of-pearl. Surely any god would respond to such lavish homage.

But these gods don't. Instead, when the messengers kiss the ground in front of his feet, and fasten to his body the gifts they've brought, the leader, the one in the red beard, wonders if these gifts are all they've brought. He asks if this is how the Aztecs greet their guests. Back in the City, before he'll hear the news, Moctezuma orders the hearts ripped out of two captives. He has their blood sprinkled on the messengers. These men, after all, have looked at the gods' faces. He sighs and shivers at the description of the cannon, how something like a ball of stone leaped from its entrails, shooting sparks, flinging fire and a smoke that smelled like rotten mud, and how the tree it aimed at shattered into splinters.

His messengers' reports tighten around Moctezuma, rather the way our story is starting to restrict our own choices, the options for selection and sequence by means of which we're composing it: the emperor is bound, whichever way he turns, by a plaiting together of contradiction, rumor, and discrepancy. As messengers, the next time, he sends out princes with gifts of gold. Now the gods smile with glee, fingering each object, snatching them from one another like monkeys, yakking away in their barbarous tongue, demanding more. The sorcerers he sends, on the final mission, never arrive. A stranger, someone they think is a drunk, waylays them. He talks and dresses as if he were from Chalco. Suddenly, his voice sounds as if he were standing far away. He tells them the City is doomed, that Moctezuma is a fool to struggle against fate. When the stranger disappears, they know it has to have been Tezcatlipoca, Lord of the Polished Judgment-Mirror. When they tell Moctezuma, he says it means the City will have to be punished. Now there's nothing to do but wait.

☙

As we turn our attention back to the Spaniards, all these shifts in perspective start to feel like a dialectical process, the self-propelled sensation of time passing. Even the Spaniards can sense it: Bernal Díaz notes how they feel that history itself is sweeping them down that causeway straight as a blade, wide as eight horses abreast, as they approach the great lakeside city. Four thousand courtiers touch earth with their right hand, kissing it, bowing, retreating. Then Moctezuma himself appears, in golden-soled sandals, preceded by princes sweeping the ground, averting their eyes, spreading rare cloths under the emperor's step, holding Cortés back lest he try to embrace him. The imperial bodyguards carry lances of fire-hardened wood tipped with skate spines. Flint glued with the blood of bats edges their wooden swords. A smokeless, fragrant tree bark burns, heating the imperial apartment. Dancers and buffoons, and tiny humpbacked clowns, bent nearly double, provide entertainment. Moctezuma smokes a couple of tubes filled with herbs, and promptly falls asleep.

Birds with long green feathers fill the imperial palace, as well as others with red feathers, white, yellow, and blue. Women clean the nests, placing eggs under birds that are brooding, harvesting the feathers. In another house the Spaniards find stone idols, and beasts of prey eating the bodies of sacrifice victims. The Spaniards eye goose quills stuffed with gold dust. They flinch at poisonous snakes with tails that ring like bells.

In the market, merchants sell food: moles and lice, the voiceless, castrated dogs they fatten, a kind of scum they net from the lake. From the top of the pyramid honoring the Aztec war-idol, voices bartering in the market leave a low hum on the air. Causeways and canoes, towers and flat-roof houses, the whole City floats. Weakened from disease and fever, Cortés studies the broad face and terrible eyes of the war-idol, the hearts of three men burning before it, the walls black with blood. He begs permission to leave an image of the Virgin there. Refused, he totters down 114 steps on abscessed legs. Everywhere he looks, men are playing games. Aztec warriors slash a tree, until it oozes white drops they roll into a ball—which they then proceed to drive back and forth, with blows from hip and thigh, the length of a great whitewashed court. Spanish soldiers gamble for gold shares with cards they've cut out of drum skins.

According to the *Crónica*, Moctezuma now orders golden necklaces hung from the necks of these gods, and wreaths of flowers put on their heads. He welcomes them to what is now their City. Their response is to put him under guard, and fire off one of their cannons. It makes a noise so huge that people run back and forth, as if they had eaten mind-numbing mushrooms. First the gods demand eggs and tortillas, chicken and drinking water and firewood and charcoal. Then they demand gold. They strip the feathers from pennants and shields, leaving only the golden frames, which they melt into ingots, along with necklaces and nose plugs, greaves and bracelets and crowns. Everything else they pile up and burn, the feathers and delicate leathers, the rare cloths and furs.

A few days later, when Moctezuma asks these gods for permission to hold the fiesta of Toxcatl, they grant it. But then, when dancers and song fill the Sacred Patio, a certain fear of the Aztec worshipers seems to overcome the gods. Anyhow they seal off the exits, attacking with swords and shields. To this day, in bark-paper paintings, the severed arms of the Aztec drummers still writhe, squirting blood, and lopped heads still roll. When dancers slashed in the abdomen try to flee, they tangle their feet in their own entrails.

Enraged, the City's entire population surrounds the Patio,

driving the attackers back into the palace where they're lodged. Moctezuma appears on a rooftop, begging his people not to resist. The elderly will suffer, and even the children, he argues. But the City seems no longer to believe in its emperor. Maybe it no longer even believes in these strange new gods. Jeers and rocks and arrows fly from below—aimed not only at the Spanish captors, but at Moctezuma as well. The citizens of Tenochtitlán are now assaulting their own emperor. Three years before, not a single one of them would have dared look him full in the face.

❧

Within weeks, the City falls. Now there begins a hideous century, one in which twenty-five million Indians die of violence or disease. Here, where the voices become at once more numerous and more anonymous, our narrative starts to unravel. No longer do primary sources recount the same events from neatly opposed perspectives. Among the voices of victims and victimizers alike, a din of contending tones threatens the two distinct convictions with which we began, that pair of world views deriving from the doctrine of soul and from that of *nahualli.* By now, Hernando Ruiz de Alarcón is writing *Treatise on the Heathen Superstitions That Live Today Among the Indians Native to This New Spain.*

A missionary priest, he needs to know when his parishioners are backsliding. So he transcribes hundreds of phrases they use to worship the old gods. We hear, in his pages, how Indians newly converted to Christianity still murmur prayers to the *nahualli:* for You we perfume the ropes of our deer snare, raveled by thrashing; we beg You to lend it Your camouflage of horns, or thorns, You who mediate between men and the Bloodless Others who never die. We can hear an old man warning a pilgrim what to beware of: hurry off, my youngest child, my bowl scrapings; take this tobacco wrapped in bark paper out to where we slit our earlobes to worship the ticklish god of battle whose captives we are.

The voices of the faithful mingle, combine, blend, and merge. They pray to their palm-leaf mats, when falling asleep, to protect them from the mockery of the sorcerer's *nahualli*, for don't their mats bear the spots of the jaguar, whose hunger prowls all four directions, and aren't the faithful prey, no matter where they hide? Chopping wood, they pray to the tree whose shins they strike, that it spare their copper axe; then they beg some *nahualli* to inhabit their tobacco, so the firewood they carry will weigh less; they even beg for the strength of the Bloodless Others, so the roads before them will lie flat.

The Aztecs' relation with the *nahualli* sounds as dynamic as it ever was. And probably it is. The source of our information, we mustn't forget, is a Roman Catholic priest, a man training other priests to eradicate pagan superstition. Ruiz de Alarcón hopes that, little by little, the *nahualli* has begun to flee before the soul, that the perishable duplicate is yielding to the immortal core. Of course, in the silence between the lines on his pages, we do hear Paternosters and Ave Marias. But his lines themselves, he hopes, record the death rattle of the *nahualli*. However, we suspect they don't. The Nahuatl phrases we read may be, of course, a guttural goodbye, as the *nahualli* retreats into the jungle, or flees to the sierra, in search of more inaccessible regions. It's far more likely, however, that the *nahualli* is simply bidding goodbye to its own traditional appearance. Already it's begun assuming a disguise.

In any event we can imagine how the landscape must look to a seventeenth-century Aztec—how the Spanish invaders carry around these pale eternities, deathless, shivering deep inside them. Wherever the Aztec looks, a certain human homogeneity goes about vanquishing the world's diversity. In town after town, as they spread across the countryside, Spaniards set up their single wooden figure of a Man, his knees torn open, his brow all thorns. Each time the conquerors topple one of the stones that used to hold shuddering hearts, the difference gets clearer to our Aztec witness. Spaniards exist. Indians correspond.

Those of us who visit Mexico today encounter a landscape riddled with ruins and museums. We even find a Spanish through which are woven Aztec terms like *zacate,* for what the Spaniard would call *hierba,* and we would call *grass.* I remember visiting, once, a seventeenth-century chapel, and studying what looked like the effigy of a saint laid out in his glass case. He seemed a perfectly ordinary Mexican religious icon, reclining in his brown robe, beard neatly combed, hands folded across his chest. It must have been ten minutes before I noticed the card at his feet, hand-lettered in elegant nineteenth-century script, identifying him as *el dios de maiz,* the god of corn. To this day he reminds me how little distance we have on the Conquest.

So when our narrative moves into the present, we hear voices that—being secondary—have been reduced to interpreting events we know now by heart, however little we understand them. Not too different, in a way, from the converts whose backsliding Ruiz de Alarcón transcribed, many of today's sources feel compelled to examine the victory of the soul, the expulsion of the *nahualli.* In his deconstructionist version of that struggle, *The Conquest of America,* Tzvetan Todorov tries to put it into a new perspective. He distinguishes "two major forms of communication, one between man and man, the other between man and the world." He adds that, while Spanish culture principally cultivates the former, the Aztecs train their attention almost exclusively on the latter. The Spaniard sees reality, Todorov suggests, as if it were a kind of perspective drawing, one in which the importance of human concerns earns them a place in the foreground, against the backdrop of the world. The Spanish mind tends to distinguish between the types of human condition, doing so on the basis of certain qualities people possess, or motives they entertain.

Todorov suggests that the Aztec, foregrounding the world, is much less interested in the varieties of the human. Rather, Aztec attention gets trained on each nuance of the nonhuman, each signal that the world emits to a trained observer. But how does Todorov's distinction apply to the struggle we've delineated, that between *nahualli* and soul? If we consider communication to be composed of the twin acts of transmitting and receiving, we can say that the Spanish attention—aimed as it is at humans—proceeds from four language activities: it receives by listening and reading; it transmits by speaking and writing. The Aztec attention, conversely, remains aimed at the nonhuman: it receives by practicing augury; it transmits with ceremony.

The *nahualli* and the soul represent, respectively, the organs of those two types of communication. The Spaniards communicate among themselves, as one eternal, indivisible soul to another. Training their attention on each other's speech, they've acquired an alphabet, a system that lets their remarks be projected over great stretches of distance or time. The Aztecs, on the other hand—born linked to the world because of their identification with the *nahualli*—have elaborated systems of divination and worship. Tenochtitlán, with all its pyramids and temples, amounts to nothing more than a giant apparatus for transmitting and receiving messages, for staying in touch with the world.

Consider, for instance, how the City worshiped Quetzalcóatl. Moctezuma apparently considered Cortés to be the Lord Himself; at least he believed the Spaniards' presence presaged the Lord's imminent return. For Moctezuma then, these bearded, strangely dressed fellows amounted to a message the world had sent the Aztecs. And the emperor, by the ceremony of giving appropriate gifts, sent a message back. For many generations, in fact, Tenochtitlán had maintained a temple to worship Quetzalcóatl, to perform the rites that made him a presence in Aztec daily life. The single priest who dwelt in the temple beat a great drum each sunset, its hoarse voice hushing people the length of the whole City. That same drum woke them each morning at sunrise, while the merchant assembled his market stall, while the housewife swept her floor.

Each year, for forty days, a slave flawless of eye and complexion impersonates Quetzalcóatl. Singing and dancing under guard in the streets, the slave knows all along that he's going to be sacrificed. If any melancholy overtakes him, his captors give him a broth they make by washing obsidian knives free of the previous dancer's blood. . . . Consider the intricate ways his followers have of adoring him; consider even the figure of the god himself: how ingenious a procedure it is that the Aztecs have devised for transmitting information to the world in which they live! Quetzalcóatl is a maneuver they use to assure the world that they are faithful, that they deserve the rain that falls, the soil that transforms dead flesh into nourishment.

So the twin acts of augury and ceremony have shaped the City. But what sense can we make of all those omens promising the return of Quetzalcóatl? Todorov attributes them to an after-the-fact desperation: to their understanding of time as an intricate series of predispositions and foreshadowings, the Aztecs would have needed to reconcile the fact of any event as unprecedented as the Conquest. Todorov argues that the prophecies, as well as the omens that yielded them, got invented soon after the fall of Tenochtitlán, in order to give the conquered the comfort of believing a little longer in a world view the Conquest was destroying.

Still, we can't avoid wondering why Todorov rejects another, more obvious explanation. Why couldn't the omens have been authentic? Why couldn't the world, in fact, have been signaling to the Aztecs? In a book entitled *Tiempo Mexicano*, Carlos Fuentes argues that they were, indeed, authentic. Of course Cortés was Quetzalcóatl, Fuentes insists. The god had returned to fulfill the ancient prophecy, to destroy the institution of human sacrifice, to bring to an end the world the Aztecs knew. And we can see how Fuentes might be right. Like Todorov,

Cortés simply didn't know how to read the world's signals, the omens which would've told him he was indeed Quetzalcóatl.

Because he treats them together in his psychohistorical study of their cults, *Quetzalcóatl and Guadalupe,* Jacques Lafaye suggests a useful pairing of these two figures. We can feel at work between them the same kind of interpretive reciprocity we noticed between the doctrine of soul and that of *nahualli:* Quetzalcóatl and the Virgin throw each other into relief. We see, in the former, an intricate concern with continuity over time. The Virgin, on the other hand, came to embody that instant at which God—in order to save human souls—intervened in the world's workings. Time itself got divided in two by the fixed point of her giving birth, an event which meant that any year, from then on, would bear a suffix—B.C. or A.D.—to focus time into the linear, into that unidirectional flow which the doctrine of the soul demanded. That's why the Virgin, when she shows up, usually has the momentary effect of stopping time.

Consider for example that December, thirteen years after the Conquest, when she appears on Tepeyac hill to Juan Diego, an Aztec peasant. She announces that she wants the bishop to build her a temple right here. She mentions that her heart aches at the suffering of her Indian children. To leave behind some proof, so that the bishop will recognize her visit as legitimate, she fills the peasant's cloak with snow and Spanish roses, and imbues it with a portrait of herself.

A hundred years later, while Ruiz de Alarcón is transcribing prayers to the *nahualli,* the faithful already are making pilgrimages to Tepeyac. At the altar honoring the Virgin of Guadalupe, they arrive singly, or in groups, to huddle below a *tilma,* a swatch of woven maguey-fiber fabric the length of a man. They see what is in fact the cloak of Juan Diego, the features of the Virgin still gazing out of it. Imagine the emotions of the newly converted, eyeing the face that stares down at them. As so many generations after them will, they feel they are her children. They're gazing, after all, at the very brow and cheekbones which appeared to Aztec peasant and Spanish bishop, from under a layer of snow and roses. Maybe they can feel her addressing the soul, this unity newly unfolded in them. Certainly they notice her face is the same color as theirs. Maybe they figure her features are dark with the effort of keeping her worshipers wholly human, of trying to banish some stubborn, elusive counterpart to everything she loves.

That depiction of the mestiza Virgin, with her mestizo worshipers kneeling before her, ought to amount to a synthesis, a kind of resolution. It ought to signal an end to what we're hearing, to provide an appropriate closure to our reenactment of the Conquest. And yet, it doesn't. For the face peering out of Juan Diego's cloak isn't, as we know, the only Mexican Virgin. Ten years before she appeared to him, she had appeared to the Spaniards. During what amounted to their only reversal of fortunes, the night they called *La Noche Triste,* when they were fighting for their lives, getting driven from Tenochtitlán, she appeared to Cortés and his men, lending them the strength to escape. And then, twenty years later, only a decade after she imbued that cloak with her own features, an Aztec nobleman heard the Virgin's voice. She commanded him to search a certain field of maguey plants, outside San Bartolo, a little way from the capital. And there our Aztec nobleman found a wooden figure of her, four feet high, the very statue which Cortés, after destroying the stone idols, had placed in the temple of Huitzilopochtli, the War-Spirit. During *La Noche Triste,* the statue was last seen protecting Captain Alvarado, who earlier had led the charge on the Sacred Patio. To our nobleman the Virgin insisted, as she had to Juan at the hill of Tepeyac, that a temple be raised, right here, to honor her.

Much of the subsequent four and a half centuries of Mexican

history seems no more than a conflict between these two manifestations of the Virgin. The one who appeared to the Aztec nobleman came to be called *La Virgen de Los Remedios*. Fair of skin, imported from Spain, she came to stand for a view of the world both aristocratic and Spanish. Cortés's men, grateful for her aid in taking Tenochtitlán, even wound up calling her *La Conquistadora*. When the other, *La Guadalupana*, appeared to an Aztec peasant, it was the force with which she announced her partiality to her "children," to Indians and the poor, that imbued her features into that cloak of rough native cloth. (*La Guadalupana*'s identification with indigenous culture was so great that even the hill on which she appeared had been sacred, first, to Tonantzin, the virgin Aztec goddess to whom were sacred corn and the earth.) Each Virgin therefore appealed to an utterly different set of loyalties. But it never did occur, to the adherents of either, to level against those loyal to the other the charge of idolatry.

Granted the polarity between them, it shouldn't surprise us to recall how, during the early nineteenth century, in the War of Independence, these two Virgins chose up sides, and came to represent the opposing factions. One banner, bearing the features of *La Guadalupana*, served the rebel Insurgents. Another, depicting *Remedios*, served the Royalists. The conflict between the two dragged on for ten years, assuming at last the ugliest characteristics of a civil war, with the surfacing of family grudges generations old, as well as the hatred of one class for another. Among her followers, each Virgin inspired an almost otherworldly loyalty. After various successes in battle, each was awarded military rank, and various promotions. (The Royalists finally conferred a generalship on *Remedios*, even dressing her in a uniform.) In skirmish after skirmish, the victors sentenced the vanquished to death by firing squad. They also put up against the wall and shot the Virgin the losers had carried into battle.

The final victory of the Insurgents, and therefore of *La Guadalupana*, brought only a pause in the many-sided antagonism that centered, by now, on the two. Yes, *La Guadalupana* had won political independence for Mexico. And yet, *Remedios* remained a resident of the country. And so did those who worshiped her. So peace brought no resolution between the wealthy and the poor, between those who felt themselves pure, and those who felt themselves mestizo. And the intervening century and three-quarters hasn't managed to lay to rest the very same animosities.

So how, then, are we going to close our reenactment of the Conquest? Far from seeming the victor, *La Guadalupana* herself begins to look more like an exercise in schizophrenia, a power struggle between different versions of the same personality. She and *Remedios,* her counterpart, start to recall the relation between the individual self and its *nahualli.* Could it be that her doubleness only represents the degree to which the Virgin failed to banish the *nahualli?* Even into the eighteenth and nineteenth centuries, she kept on driving it from cities and towns, but only at the cost of acquiring even more counterparts to herself: the Virgin of San Juan de Los Lagos, the Virgin of Zapopan. . . .

Unlike our earlier material, these legends about the Virgin have no source. Or rather, they have thousands of sources. They'll show up in flyers that try to raise funds for a new chapel, and later get alluded to during the remarks that dedicate it: they thrive in the kinds of speech that her different images draw from those devoted to her. Different versions of her multiply, to this day, automatically as cells that leap outward in all directions, from a single source. Yet often enough, in these scattered impressions, we think we catch a glimpse of the Virgin herself. It was the beam of her own single, unifying will that refracted her. In spreading over the landscape, she broke into a whole spectrum of interests and associations, ubiquitous as harsh sunlight attacking the stubborn prism of Aztec belief.

When I watch the Virgin of Zapopan get transported, every fall, through the Guadalajara streets, bricklayer and banker alike tugging the rope tied to the front axle of her sedan, I know she amounts to nothing more than an eighteenth-century porcelain head attached to a body made of cornhusks. Half a million people throng the sidewalks for five miles, cheering as she proceeds from the cathedral to her basilica. Sometimes I even climb a rooftop to catch a glimpse of her, eighteen inches high, a scrap of pale silk seeming to float above the applause and the smiles. It's easy to forget, at such a moment, how the multiplicity of her selves derives from forces lying way beyond the unity that she claims to represent. She's a signal, after all, that we receive every year from the world.

THE TOUR GUIDE

Mi amarga y continua leyenda de los
detestables libros de las caballerías.
Ya conozco sus disparates y sus embelecos. . . .
—Don Quijote

Fictional narrative, some historians think, may not have existed much before *Don Quijote*. Indeed, the narrative in Virgil or Homer might have looked in 1500 very much like argument, or more specifically, like an illustration of stages in a soul's progress. We can only speculate about the changes in attitude that made us crave what Ezra Pound, in the second decade of this century, knew our age demanded, "a prose kinema." For finally it is the cinematic, the kinetic, quality of narrative that attracts us. As frame replaces frame, the characters shudder into motion, their story rippling like a deck of illustrated cards.

133

It is all sleight of hand of course. Yet it does leave us examining our own lives. And way too often they seem less than coherent. Sometimes the separate moments blur together. Other times they seem to freeze, paralyzing us with boredom. We know that even when the cards are shuffled and dealt, spread before us out of sequence, we can still draw conclusions from them, infer former sequences, and even gain insights not possible otherwise. But why do we find the narrative version so seductive? Two different aspects of narrative account for our fascination with it. First, as we reach the end of a narrative, we often feel that its events have followed one another with a certain inevitability. We feel comforted by the illusion that at last we "understand" what happened, which events were causes, which were effects. Those who blame narrative for giving the reader an overly simplified view of life keep focusing on this aspect of it. They are also missing the point.

The second aspect of narrative suggests a subtler yet far more serious accusation. For notice that no matter how inevitable they seem in retrospect, the events of a story seem enough in doubt to keep us reading. It is the principle of suspense that first attracts us to a story, then keeps us reading to the end. Thus narrative may or may not give us an overly simplified view of life. But it does give us the impression that at any given moment what happens is beyond our anticipation, and thus beyond our control. But why should we like to believe that we are powerless? Perhaps we like to believe that forces beyond our control lend our lives a significance that quite transcends our importance as individuals: believing it allows our lives to represent those impersonal trends and tendencies that, for us, have replaced the gods as sources of meaning.

We judge our experience by narrative standards: beforehand, it feels unpredictable; afterward, it seems to have been inevitable. And so, like a friend with whom I got a little drunk some years ago on my birthday, we feel half-cheated. A remarkable poet, Ted had grown up in Rhode Island. And change though his work might over the years, a certain New England quilting-bee reserve presided over, and bound together, the fundamentally angular patchwork it all remained. His career had begun, or nearly so, with a hip sonnet sequence from a commercial publisher. By the time we met, all the important awards had evaded his maybe too diffident grasp. Now he lived with his wife and two children on the second, or was it third, floor of an old brick building on St. Mark's Place, down on the Lower East Side.

Was it only the battleship gray of stair and landing that lent a cramped feel to the sunlight, that April afternoon? We cut around the corner to a Puerto Rican liquor store. The gray-haired owner nodded at Ted, and rang up our fifth of Cuervo. *Y no habrá descuento pa' el turista Mexicano?* I asked him. *Para la otra vez que vengas, mi hijo, ya está.* Ted wondered, back outdoors, what it was we'd said. Friendly banter about an ethnic discount, I replied—you could call it professional courtesy. Back in his apartment, coffee cup of tequila on forefinger, the Chesterfield between his lips dribbling ash through his beard, he toyed with our conversation's new theme, that of professional courtesy. There was something, something I was supposed to do for my career, after *The Sonnets* came out. But I didn't do it. What was it? I asked. He looked out the window. He said, I never knew.

I was living in those days in the Bronx. And teaching on Monday nights a single class that met forty miles, more or less, south of Detroit. Yes, Detroit. Five hundred fifty miles of driving—eleven hundred round trip—each week. I'd walk into walls, forgetting where I was. I began to feel a certain atemporal quality taking over those days. Any given moment lay closest not to those which preceded and followed, but rather to some other, often chronologically far removed, some moment with which it struck a compelling angle. Voices, the feelings they held, whole scenes even—days otherwise far apart in my life began to reflect one another, like mirrors carrying a bit of news across the North American desert. How I'd taken such a job, how I'd come even to be living in New York—it all receded to a background now too faint to reconstruct. Or to matter.

Ted was already dead a couple of months when I learned he was gone, from the first of what would be several conflicting tales about how it happened. When a friend sat me down and quietly said amphetamine had killed him, I didn't know quite how to feel. Back from a visit to other friends, I had flown in just a few hours earlier from Guadalajara. That very morning I had visited don Chino. He was seventy-five years old. As light and carbon monoxide spilled through his living-room window, we chatted about the Russians killing how many passengers was it in midair. Maybe they even had a few seconds in which to get used to the notion of being dead, don Chino thought aloud. These days, the world seemed run by capricious thugs. Thank God his own life had been, in however slight a way, the result of his own choices. At fifteen he had fled on foot, from a poor and tiny village high in the Sierra, the two hundred miles to Guadalajara. He studied for the priesthood, but lost the faith. He became yardboy to a politician who, in kindness, secured him a similar job with the president of the state university. The arrangement was that Chino would go through medical school while living in the president's garage, earning his keep in the yard. But in his last year of studies the government changed and with it the governor, who in turn named another man president of that university. So don Chino decided to drive a bus. He married. He had children. And now one morning nearly half a century later, he sat savoring the irony of it all: nineteen years of schooling, and I drive a bus every day the thirty kilometers from Guadalajara to Magdalena.

Ted had the most agile voice I ever heard. Rather small for a man his size—nearly three hundred pounds, with the shoulders and neck and thighs of an ex–running back—his voice had grown deft as a hummingbird. It was mainly New England, though not as to accent, but rather in the intimate camera angles he could wring from it. I never heard him speak loudly. It seemed a voice from somewhere people lived forever in close-up to one another. It could take offense, but very quietly. It could spring a punch line out of nowhere. While don Chino's voice, not quite the contrary, rang with all that was amicable. His were the hand-carved good manners of the beginning of our century: no feel of coldness from him, at all. He simply hailed from that one country which runs, north and south, from Calgary to Guadalajara, where men understand distance as respect. Anyway, try to imagine somewhere we could stand to hear them talk to one another, the Irish-American poet, the Mexican traveling man.

Don Chino, I am happy to report, remains alive and well. I saw him but a few months ago. Indeed, a narrative would surely return to him here. For narrative amounts to an agreement, much like that of professional courtesy: with the gift of a story, the narrator binds him- or herself to us, intensifying the degree of trust between us. If we trust enough to tolerate long and puzzling digressions, we do so in hopes the story will take on, finally, that inevitability which leaves the whole more vivid than whatever events compose it. When I remember Ted telling me the tale of Delmore Schwartz dying, begging for help in the hall of some hotel, I feel the entire relationship between us getting more vivid.

Ted was riddled with digressions that afternoon, already some while after our April drink. As yellow leaves blew across Washington Square, he joked whether there were none or few of them. I must have complained at the lack of animal life in the city, for he prescribed long walks through museums and galleries. Paintings are the native bird life of New York, I remember he said. But we parted, somehow, with gruff words. I think I clumsily hoped aloud something about him being careful with amphetamines. That I look to my own habits, and in a hurry— that was all his reply. I never saw him again.

I think Ted felt above all a need to be quite private about his feelings. As if no one could intuit how he felt. And yet, like nineteenth-century maps that produced but a nearer and nearer approximation of some continent no one could glimpse entirely, oblique versions of our friends do leap at us. Ted the drinker, Ted the Catholic. Who knows from how many vantage points the different corners of him resolve, now into profile, and now to three-quarters.

But they do. Just as parts of Chino's life feel ironic both to him and to us, so Ted resolves into figure and ground, continent and ocean. His remarks isolate him in time, forming with one another the same kind of compelling angles we feel certain moments of our own lives forming. Even a single remark can shed, like a pebble in water, that widening, binding ripple pattern we recognize as character. Only last month, appropriately enough, I visited the woman who taught me to read and write. Indeed it was from her that I learned to consider moments as premises which, however widely scattered, yield hidden conclusions— the way one sagebrush, no different from a hundred others, will explode with pheasant wings. Now she lay in a rest home, dying of pancreatic cancer, her hair white as her pillowcase. She'd taken out her teeth to vomit, which left her cheekbones even higher, more fragile. I just don't know what's doing this, she apologized.

She began to recall the two-room school in which she'd taught for fifty years. Names I hadn't heard since I was ten sprang from her, each triggering my memory of a small pale face. Most of my classmates now held decent factory jobs, or had married the patient and dinnerpail-reliable kind of man who did. Though one was a civil engineer, and another, in Alaska now, a teacher. She had fought the board of education once to keep a big feebleminded boy in school. They thought he was too moody and dangerous, ever since the day he lost his temper with her and she, at one hundred pounds, had to throw him three times in a row, in a fair fight, right before all the schoolchildren. People wondered, she said, if she regret-ted never having married. Those twelve-hour days, the drippy noses, the muddy feet. But didn't people realize she'd do it all over again, without changing a thing?

In a lifetime each of us makes, at most, a handful of perfectly truthful remarks. A phrase here, a single word right there, they reveal us to anyone ready to listen—not so much to listen to the story we're telling, but rather to how one remark throws another into relief. Few people pay attention to others that way; and fewer yet, to themselves. But consider the grip such listeners do maintain on us. Consider even the public scribes that perch outside any Mexican market. One by one, illiterate men approach: for a fee, a fellow with a typewriter will write down whatever news or need has driven them to him. One man's story will take the form of a letter to those waiting back home. Another comes ready to mumble a marriage proposal. And yet no matter how often a man rehearses his message, when he realizes perfect strangers now will be able to read his thoughts, he starts to stammer. Oblique angles surface in what he has to say.

We practice two kinds of hearing. At any moment, we may be listening to a story; or we may be listening through it to suggestions that lie beyond it. The latter, of course, is how you have been reading my remarks. As my words pass before your eyes, your presence makes me feel like a fellow I met once, years ago, when I worked leading tours in Mexico. Taking a group one weekend to a small state museum, in a little town in the mountains, I found standing at the door a man who seemed at least in his eighties. He identified himself as our official guide.

Clean and patched though it was, his uniform might have belonged thirty years before to an airline pilot. Did he speak English? Yes, of course he spoke the English. If my friends and I would be but good enough to step this way. Before a glass case full of potsherds, he began a speech in some language I'd never heard before. The people on the tour got to wondering, soon enough, what he was saying. In Spanish I'd ask and he'd answer in Spanish, only to lapse again into that curious patter.

At length a word or two of what he said began to leak into my mind. It was English alright. Of course it was. Without understanding a word, he had phonetically memorized the text of what now began to sound like a standard authority on the crafts

of that county. Sure enough, I could hear the very words of the
scholar—a fellow probably dead for years—finding their way
through all that accent, out to where we waited, on limestone
benches, smoking and slapping mosquitoes, wondering what it
was that our lives meant.

LAS AVENTURAS

I spent the most introspective year of my life riding around in the back seat of a Mexican highway-patrol car. The two officers up front looked like Jack Webb and Ben Alexander, from the Dragnet TV series out of the midfifties. But these were the late seventies. And we three patrolled not Los Angeles, but rather the back roads and small towns of Jalisco, outside Guadalajara.

The shorter and darker of the two, my compadre René did the driving. His holster and shoes bore a mirrorlike polish. Shirt and trousers tailored by hand, he carried himself with a certain intensity, a blend of curtness and eloquence. His partner, Vicente, nicknamed El Güero, stood nearly six feet tall, with red hair, blue eyes, and the rumpled, bemused air of a man just awakened from a nap.

Whatever other duties brought us together during the week, Friday and Saturday nights, from eight till one in the morning, we patrolled for drunks, or for speeders. As the squad car nosed along through the dark, every couple of hours, behind a big *huizache* bush, we'd stop to pee. An undemanding kind of talk, aimless enough to kill time, filled the air. Back and forth from women to baseball, our conversations wandered until, every so often, without a signal, we'd stop to stretch and relieve ourselves. Even when one of the three didn't feel the urge, he'd accompany the other two. A remark René muttered one night while dropping his zipper seems, all these years later, to explain the relationship we enjoyed: *no hay mexicano que mee solo.* No Mexican pees alone.

My friends worked well together. The stolid, taciturn Güero offset René's vibrant energy: while the latter intimidated, the former invited trust. Rare indeed was the lawbreaker who didn't end up confessing to one or the other. Faced with so fortuitous a pairing of "good cop" and "bad cop," the factory worker who'd downed a few too many beers, or taken a corner a bit too fast, must have sensed in the first few minutes how futile it was to protest his innocence. I often wondered, though, what such a fellow must have thought of me, the guy in the back seat, listening, taking notes.

Not quite as fair of skin as the Güero, I'm considerably taller. Then as now, I favored Levi's and running shoes in brands that clearly marked me as coming from the United States. And yet, through accidents both of upbringing and interest, I sound Mexican when I speak Spanish, and am pretty nearly bicultural. So I must have seemed, to the newly arrested factory worker, both enigmatic and vaguely threatening. More than one such fellow must have wondered what the hell I was doing there.

I was supposed to be writing a book. On leave from a teaching position in the Pacific Northwest, I'd followed the woman to whom I was married down to New Orleans, where she'd acquired a professorship. As the year drew on, the marriage deteriorated. One day it occurred to me to visit René, whom I'd met years before, and to whose next-to-oldest son I was godfather. The visit that I'd meant to take a few days wound up lasting a month. And in a matter of weeks, I was back to visit him again. More and more, it seemed, the only place I could concentrate—the only area free of interference—became the little town where René lived, and the back seat of the squad car he drove.

The town was named El Salto, after a waterfall in the river that ran beside it—or rather, that once had run beside it. For the last ten years or so, only a trickle of water had flowed in the lily-choked bed, under the rusty bridge that led from El Salto to Juanacatlán, the neighboring town. The river had declined during the same period that saw, on either side of the highway we patrolled, a twentyfold increase in the number of small industrial plants which, in turn, had attracted workers in ever greater numbers. Now both towns kept edging out, subdivision by subdivision, through the pastures that surrounded them.

One by one the factories had diverted the river for their own use. More specifically, they assembled products which then got shipped north to the United States. The drying up of the river, the arrival of hundreds of workers from outside—features such as these kept El Salto forever reminded of its status as an economic colony, both dependent on and resentful of its wealthy English-speaking neighbors to the north. The last ten years had seen El Salto's skyline sprout a forest of TV antennas, each of which drew out of the air every night many hours of what once had been prime-time U.S. programming. Long outdated, dubbed in Spanish, Kojak and Matt Dillon enforced every night the laws and customs by which Saltenos formed their impressions of cities like New York and Dodge, places separated from them not just by a wealth created, in part, here in El Salto, but as well by deep differences in social structure, and in religion.

To the town, naturally, I represented that wealth and power the influence of which were changing its life forever. No one used the term *gringo*. Rather, they called people from the United States *gabachos*, a term that Spaniards apply to the French and which, in Mexico, distinguishes the U.S. gringo from his British or Canadian counterpart. So my citizenship lent to my relations with the Saltenos a kind of cutting edge. No matter what degree of intimacy we might achieve, a gesture or tone always surfaced, at the last moment, to remind me that I was a guest. Share though I might the exasperations and triumphs of daily life, someone was always sure to point out that, whenever I wanted to, I was free to leave behind the potholes and dust, the diesel fumes and the cardboard shacks of a town that, like the country to which it belonged, was growing too fast to be entirely healthy.

These were the conditions under which I helped René and the Güero patrol the Jaliscan highways. Though I came along for the ride, they, of course, were working for a living. However much our nights in the squad car represented, to me, an escape from the grip of a dying marriage, each of my friends was supporting a wife and several children, not to mention a girlfriend or two. Their salaries were minimal. From what amounted to no more than a couple of hundred dollars a month, they had to buy their weapons and uniforms, squad car and gasoline. But neither counted on the patrol to pay him a living wage: the Güero, with the help of his wife, ran an auto-parts store at the same edge of town where René, across the street, operated an auto-repair shop. The truly lucrative end of police work consisted in the practice of accepting "considerations," or making "arrangements." *La mordida* Mexicans call the small bribe offered an official to secure a favor. The word means, literally, *a bite;* it brings to mind the image of a dog protecting his territory. Many generations of adaptation have left the practice ritualized as a handshake.

I remember one of the drunken drivers we apprehended. A young man of twenty-five or so, he'd managed to lose control of his Volkswagen beetle, plunging it to the bottom of the ten-foot culvert that paralleled the road shoulder. We arrived on a bright Sunday afternoon, about four o'clock. He was just climbing up the steep embankment, hand over hand. Dressed in a shirt and tie, blazer and tan slacks, he obviously had come from a wedding reception or a christening. Catching sight of René's uniform, he apparently decided to brazen his way out of his difficulty. "Good afternoon, officer, I certainly do appreciate your

prompt attention. Indeed, my own cousin is a highway patrol-
man, so I better than most people know how deeply a moment's
inattention can leave a fellow depending on the skill and tact of
trained professionals such as yourself. . . ." Only the large urine
stain on his pants leg gave him away.

As the youngster prattled on and on, René's silence was that
of a tomb. He frisked the kid for weapons; he impounded his
automobile. Firmly the Güero put him in the back of our squad
car. All the while the four of us headed for town, the young
man kept wheedling and importuning, wondering aloud if we
couldn't work out some "arrangement." He began by offering a
hundred pesos. My friends didn't even glance back. An offer of
two hundred followed, only to elicit the same lack of response.
When finally, clutched in shaking fingers, a single five-hundred
peso note made its way from back seat to front, the Güero
pocketed the bill. With a warning to appear for arraignment
the following Wednesday, René deposited our "prisoner" on a
corner.

As we drove off, the two of them trained on me a little lecture
in the social utility of the *mordida*. I suppose you think, René
said, that the kid has bought his way out of trouble. But notice
that he hasn't. His five hundred pesos have secured him only
what you up north would call "bail." If he doesn't appear next
Wednesday, he'll lose his car, and we'll issue a warrant for his
arrest. The five hundred pesos he paid for three days of liberty
will buy us a tank of gas, as well as a decent dinner. And the
three of us, added the Güero, are what keep the highways of
Jalisco safe.

I had to admit that they had a point. The convention of the
mordida seemed to work at least as well as its far more intri-
cate counterpart to the north. So within a few weeks, when
we apprehended a very different drunken driver, I could better
appreciate the fine gradations of judgment that the system de-
manded of an officer. The second driver had made a real mess.
At eight o'clock on a week night, he'd hit one of the buses that
carried factory workers to and from their shift. When we ar-

rived, a couple of passengers lay stretched on the road shoulder with cuts and bruises. Soon the driver himself sat in the back of our patrol car, offering a thousand pesos, then two thousand, and then five. His speech was thick. He even drooled a little, insisting that his brother, a Guadalajara lawyer, was good for the money. René and the Güero ignored his entreaties, and kept on filling out paperwork. Within an hour we had him behind bars.

The difference in how the two drunks got treated owed, in part, to the fact that the second was a repeat offender. The injuries suffered by the bus passengers would've made it necessary to take into our confidence the other investigating officers, as well. But mostly, the second fellow went to jail because my friends considered him dangerous to others, and thought he should be taught a lesson. Over dinner that night, they explained the factors limiting the *mordida* system. If the highways became overdangerous, they argued, the two of them stood to lose their jobs. A kind of natural balance existed, they wanted me to understand.

As the dinner drew to a close, the Güero wanted to know why, by the way, I kept writing down what we said and did. René explained that I was a writer. You mean you're actually writing a book? the Güero demanded, incredulous. I said I was. Do you plan to put your compadre and me in it? I said I might. The Güero thought for a long time. Right there, over the tacos and soda pop, I could feel my relationship with him change forever. From that moment on, whenever the three of us climbed in the squad car, the Güero would aim a sly grin at me, only to wonder aloud, *otro capítulo?* Another chapter? After a couple more weeks of collecting bribes and peeing on plants, he even had a title for what I was writing. He suggested I call it *Las Aventuras de Dos Guardianes Cumplidos y Sacrificados de la Ley Mexicana con un Gabacho*. The Adventures of Two Hard-Working, Self-sacrificing Guardians of the Mexican Law with a Gabacho.

Little by little, my waking hours came to revolve around the police duties of my friends. I'd stay up with them till midnight, patrolling, or propped gossiping on chairs on the sidewalk. By nine in the morning I'd be in the office to help with paperwork, or to type the endless forms that the bureaucracy required. The office itself was a single room with a concrete floor, its concrete walls bare except for a current calendar. A single naked light bulb dangled from the ceiling. There appeared at the door, every morning, the factory workers or cowboys who needed to renew a driver's license often as much as a year out of date.

From noon to four we'd shut down, have a long lunch, and take a nap. We'd open the office again from four to seven. Our schedule varied because of the constant demand that wrecks made on our time. Indeed, at whatever moment news of an accident might arrive—by phone, or more often by word of mouth—we had to drop all we were doing and rush to the scene. Even the simplest of collisions, with no one injured, with property damage minimal, obligated us to hours of filling out forms, interviewing witnesses, studying skid marks, and drawing maps. Sometimes weeks would pass without an accident, only to be followed by three, or even four, in a single day.

No two wrecks were alike. They shared only the properties of occurring at an unexpected hour, and of having about them a certain gaudy, preposterous quality. Once, from a collision between two trucks bearing cases of empty Pepsi bottles, I saw fifty yards of highway covered six inches deep in shattered glass. Another time I watched a dozen men and women in evening clothes stand barefoot, ankle deep in the muddy road shoulder, relaying to each other buckets of fuel oil, pouring them into the empty tanker they'd rented. Having hurried directly to the accident from a wedding, they were draining the overturned tanker in order to keep the poor from pilfering their investment.

At four o'clock in the morning, in fact, of the day that began my fortieth year on this earth, a shout flew at my window from the cobblestone street below. A wreck had occurred about twelve kilometers west of town. We were dressed and at the scene in twenty minutes, only to find no one there. A car with a bashed front fender, engine still warm, stood beside the road. In the culvert lay a dead heifer, her front legs snapped, flies on her eyes. Already the car's trunk lid bore scratch marks, from where someone had tried to pry it open to steal the spare tire and the jack.

Identifying the car's driver became the easy part. Within hours we learned it had been rented, in Guadalajara, from an agency which gave us his name. We issued a warrant for his arrest, and turned our attention to the heifer. To whom did she belong? Since her owner was liable for the damages caused by her wandering loose on the highway, finding out wasn't going to be easy. With a pocketknife I sawed from her flank the patch of hide that carried the brand. It was maddeningly slow work. As the sun came up and mosquitoes sang, I began to sweat, and to tug in frustration at her. The legs dangled where they were broken, lending a coy, limp quality to her bulk. She exuded a sickly-sweet odor of grass and manure that clung, days later, after countless hot and soapy showers, to my hair and to my skin, stubborn as a cheap cologne.

When we asked, none of the local cowboys admitted recognizing the brand. Nope, never saw it, they'd mumble and eye the horizon, spitting just beyond their bony, sandal-clad feet. So we borrowed a tow truck and winched her aboard; we drove her to Chuy, who owned the truck, and once had been a butcher. The next day he sent us a big aluminum platter heaped with the choicest cuts of flank and loin. But we gave most of it away, after it sat in the kitchen a few days, since the refrigerator had broken down, weeks before. Even today, patting a meatloaf together, I shiver at the odor that ground beef imparts to my palms.

The reluctance of the cowboys to help us identify the heifer's owner was typical. Like poor people on this side of the border, Saltenos distrusted and avoided their police. Therefore the social life that René and the Güero enjoyed involved, for the most part, getting together with other cops. The Thursday afternoon lunches were notorious. By noon, in a picnic area beside a little-traveled highway, the brother officers began assembling. By two the dozen picnic tables were full of sixty or so uniformed men. Plates of enchiladas and *carnitas* lay before them, as well as a seemingly endless line of tequila and brandy bottles. More than once I wondered who could be left to patrol the roads. The prospect of sixty half-drunken Mexican cops, laughing and joking and (naturally!) comparing pistols and tales of the trade, can only call to mind, to a U.S. audience, a scene of almost unmitigated *machismo*. (As if the United States had to expropriate a concept from a "foreign" language to analyze the shortcomings of maleness!) And yet I found, after awhile, that the concept of *machismo* served the Mexican officers more as a target of ridicule than as any guide to behavior. They delighted in stories deflating their own importance. Their sense of the absurd kept the proceedings free of any pomposity.

One of the best stories (maybe my own prejudice should be excused) came from René and the Güero. It involved their apprehending once, before I began riding with them, a speeder on a powerful motorcycle. He'd flown through town doing seventy or so. They chased him in the patrol car to an intersection where, when he tried to turn, he lost control and spilled, ending up in a pasture. As the Güero approached him, he leaped to his feet and threw a neat left hook, depositing the surprised Güero right on the seat of his pants. René tackled the guy from behind, threw an arm lock on him, and shouted to the Güero to spray him with the U.S. Army surplus tear gas they carried, unable to afford the more expensive chemical Mace. As the Güero approached and took aim, the prisoner ducked, sending the stream directly at René's nose and eyes, flattening him with a fit of gasping and tears. The Güero's second effort managed to catch in the breeze, and fly back in his own face, leaving both my friends stretched on their backs, disgusted, gasping for breath. The criminal by now thought their police work so hilarious, he doubled over with laughter, after which he helped the arresting officers up and into their squad car, and drove them into town, where he promptly turned himself in.

It was scarcely the type of story one would expect from a pair of fellows intent on enhancing their reputation as humorless

instruments of power. At each rendition of it, the other offi-
cers cheered and howled, and sought to match it with tales of
their own ignominy. In fact, those peals of official laughter re-
main for me the most durable sound from all the months I spent
there. Great whoops and yelps of glee rising through the willow
boughs seemed at once both to mock and to let us share a deep
uneasiness we felt at being male. It was as if we belonged to a
secret brotherhood, a clan knit by bonds of mutual recognition.
However tough or efficient a fellow might seem anywhere else,
here, tucked away in a grove in the sunlight, each of us could
admit that he often felt plain ridiculous. René, I thought, had an
apt expression for what it was we shared: *no somos machos,* he'd
grin and glance around, *pero somos muchos.* We're not machos,
but there's a lot of us.

Ten years have passed since I last rode in the squad car with
my friends. And a decade's perspective allows me now to con-
sider issues that, in those days, I barely could recognize. I keep
wanting to reintroduce myself into those evenings that by now,
as part of the past, lie sealed off from all but my own endless
speculation. To one of those newly arrested drunks or speeders
whose paranoia my presence aroused, I want to explain what
I'm doing there. No, I'm not from the CIA, I want to answer the
question that he doesn't dare ask. I'm not even connected with
the drug trade. I'm only a kind of apprentice. I'm down here
learning how to tolerate being a man.

I certainly needed to learn. My marriage, before that year
was out, withered into acrimony, and then into separation. My
wife felt duties such as washing clothes and cooking weren't fit
work for a man. Or she'd accuse me of lacking skill. I'd used
too little fabric softener, or maybe the wrong type. I'd forgotten
to rinse the lid of the soup can before I opened it. Whatever her
objection, my response made it worse. I could manage only the
kind of silence that poised between sulking and sympathizing.
I'd slip on a smelly shirt, and go buy dinner for two at Burger
Chef. Sooner or later, I'd always end up perched in the back of
that squad car, next to the kind of fellow to whom, all these
years later, I finally get around to explaining my presence.

I'm down here, I tell him, because this life of riding around, talking about baseball and women, peeing on plants in the dark, keeps in perspective a certain tired absurdity—that of belonging to some group credited with exercising a power which it rarely, in fact, possesses. I'm male in somewhat the same way that I'm *gabacho:* only by the expectations of others, not by any explicit choice I've made. My brother officers entertain their own motives for being here. They do have women and children to support. Maybe they even think they have a power to exercise. Yet life along the roadside provides example after example of just how shabby and momentary our power truly is. People react to how we look, as well as to what we do, in a manner which demands that we do what we do, and look the way we look. Incongruous as the wrecks we observe, we shake down wet-leg drunks, and gather in secret meeting places to laugh at our own ineptitude. Our usefulness lies in that degree to which we do manage to maintain things—the highway, our own lives, or those of others—in bearable conditions. We do, after all, imprison the worst offenders. Sometimes we even eat road kill.

Consider this business of being male, I continue. Already the suspect with whom I share the back seat wears the uneasy, wide-eyed look of a man who knows perfectly well that he's being imagined. His very existence, he knows, serves as nothing more than a pretext for the stream of remarks now trained upon him. And I, for my part, feel a little silly. In a dim, reflexive way I even understand that at the moment he and I are assuming the usual roles taken, in diplomatic dialogue, by the countries we represent. But none of that matters, anymore. By now I can't let the topic go.

Learning to be a male, I insist, obliges a fellow only to master the art of keeping a straight face, the knack of maintaining a show of indifference when trapped between the deadly and the slapstick. Take, for example, the other night when we chased the drug dealer. René and I are patrolling the park, where a traveling carnival set up its cotton-candy stands and peep shows. A hundred or so children are running loose, shrieking,

from one attraction to another. As we ease the squad car over in
the direction of a sports car with Texas plates, the latter pulls off
the road nonchalantly, under the trees, nosing its way through
the children. As we follow, it speeds up. When suddenly it bolts
for a back road, nearly flattening a couple of kids, René touches
off the siren and red light, gas pedal grinding on the floorboard.
When we accelerate to forty, though, we cross a big boulder that
rips open the gas tank's bottom. By the time we reach the edge
of town, the squad car shudders to a halt, drained of gas. So
we watch our fugitive's taillights disappear down a gravel road.
And yet, the *cabrón* has outsmarted himself, René announces.
That's a dead-end road.

The guy probably deals drugs, René continues, so we have to
assume he has a weapon. While René sets off on foot to flush
him out, I'm to wait for the fellow to come by. If I hear shots, I'm
to take him out with the *fusca,* a semiautomatic .22 rifle, stock
and barrel trimmed short, adapted a month ago in someone's
garage so that now it will fire on automatic. René tells me to
pretend I'm in a basketball game shooting free throws. Try, he
says, to put all fifty rounds from the clip right in his windshield.

So there I stand in the dark, beside a deserted Jaliscan road,
ready to kill a stranger with a homemade weapon that—since
it has never been fired—may blow up in my hands. As the min-
utes drag by, I know that for the rest of my life I'll keep on
referring back to this very scene. It will remain for as long as I
live a standard against which I measure moments of danger and
foolishness. Even two hours later, when the fellow still hasn't
passed, and René returns to admit that this road maybe isn't
quite such a dead end after all; even a month later, when René
happens to see the sports car at a roadside taco stand, and con-
fronts the owner, a scared Chicano from Texas, who admits he
fled only because his license tabs had expired: no matter how
much time goes by, I can't shake from my mind the incongruity
of that moment, its qualities equally lethal and ludicrous, its
heightening of the deadly burlesque that manliness really is.

But by now he's grown decidedly uncomfortable, the fellow

I've imagined into place beside me. What pleasure can there be, after all, in sitting beside a dark road in the back of a squad car listening to a foreigner half again your size rave about the madness of masculinity? I'd better let him go. The only charge I have against him, really, is that of constituting an appropriate audience for my remarks—a charge he can scarcely confess to. (Madness, more than masculinity, seems to him to be my problem.)

No, I myself had better confess that I fled to El Salto—and now have returned, if only in memory—only in order to write. So what if the book of poems I wrote came out, years ago, to the minor but gratifying kind of notice that such events attract? René appears in it only once; it mentions the Güero not at all. But writing it represented my excuse to ride in the squad car, to share with my friends the isolation of knowing we were terribly different from everything people took us for.

And what, after all, do these very paragraphs represent, if not my own uneasiness at the prevailing disguises of gender? So now when I return in my mind to the refuge that El Salto once represented, I can see that the marriage I fled had been over already for months, and maybe even for years. It only remained for my wife and me to admit it: she and I simply weren't the right audience for each other. Admitting that we weren't was what kept me coming back to El Salto.

The town absorbed my attention with a stubborn ambiguity, a drawing power rather like the fascination I must have exerted on the Saltenos themselves. In fact I studied that place so hard that, all these years later, I think I could reconstruct it: the mare whose hooves clattered on cobblestone, every morning at two, prowling the alley under my window; the toilet-bowl stench of the sulfur the denim factory emptied into the river on Tuesday nights; don Pablo, so old and deaf that you had to shout to him over the counter of his store that you wanted cigarettes, only to have him scold you for shouting, and insist that he wasn't deaf, and ask what it was that you wanted on your sandwich. I spent whole afternoons alone, damning the institution of marriage, propped between the concrete mermaids supporting the roof of the plaza bandstand, eyeing palm trees so tall and skinny they seemed to support the sky.

Even now, in the midst of a thriving marriage, three thousand miles and ten years removed from those afternoons, I sometimes catch myself coming up with one more feeble excuse to return, in my mind, to El Salto. My wife and I both insist that, before all else, we treat each other as each other. Only in a playful, tongue-in-cheek way do she and I ever relate as male and female. A couple of times a summer, I'll insist on cooking for friends I've invited to dinner. I pull the barbecue grill into the yard, and set to slapping a couple of pounds of ground beef into shape. Once again I sniff on my palms that smell of dead heifer, the sweet-sick whiff of raw flesh, that odor of our general and unisex mortality. We all have a few beers. And I tell to friends who've heard them before my best El Salto stories.

How was it that I ever managed to say goodbye to that town? The week when I was supposed to leave lurched unexpectedly into view, sudden as one of those wrecks that punctuated our nights and days. If I didn't leave, anyhow, I'd better plan on staying forever. So I did return to the teaching job I'd held, by then, for fifteen years. I left that wife in New Orleans. And I left El Salto to be no more than the scene of a summer visit or two, as well as this constant tangle of sense impressions snaring my memory.

Anyhow, the last Sunday René and the Güero and I set out patrolling, we hadn't gone a mile before we found a wreck. A couple of fenders dangled, dented. The drivers were squaring off on the road shoulder, filling the air with blame and blasphemies. As René and the Güero calmed them down, and interviewed the witnesses, I stood out in the road, directing traffic. A Volvo station wagon bearing Iowa plates eased to a stop beside me. From it emerged a blond fellow, thirty or so years of age, who eyed me and asked, in an English thick with Scandinavian accent, whether or not I spoke English. I said I did. Enormously relieved, he smiled and announced that he and his new bride had graduated, the week before, from medical school in Iowa City. Before returning to Stockholm to open a practice, they meant to treat themselves to a little honeymoon in Irapuato. But somehow, back in Guadalajara, they'd taken a wrong turn. Could I help out with directions?

I had to ask the Güero how to get to Irapuato. As I turned back, interpreting his directions, I could see the Swede was troubled. He wanted to ask something else, but wasn't sure if he should. Finally unable to resist, he cleared his throat and wondered aloud if all Mexican cops spoke English as well as I did. From somewhere years off in the future, I could feel myself listening hard, waiting, anticipating my own response. And then, for an instant, I formed with myself a kind of invisible brotherhood. Of course we do, I smiled, clapping his shoulder. We all speak English at least as well as I'm talking it to you now. But many of us, you understand, remain a little bit shy. You need to talk real loud. Bite out your words, I told him, like you mean them. Whatever it is you're saying, talk like a man.

Philip Garrison is an associate professor of English at Central Washington State University. He has written three books, including *Away Awhile,* a poetry collection.